Other Books
by Jean Scott

*The Frugal Gambler*
*More Frugal Gambling*
*Frugal Video Poker*
*Frugal Video Poker Scouting Guide*


Other Frugal Products

*Frugal Video Poker Software*
*Frugal Video Poker Strategy Cards*

# Tax Help
# for Gamblers

# Tax Help
# for Gamblers

## Poker & Other
## Casino Games

**Jean Scott, The Frugal Gambler
& Marissa Chien, Enrolled Agent**

**Foreword by Phil Gordon,
Professional Poker Player**

HUNTINGTON PRESS
LAS VEGAS, NEVADA

**Tax Help for Gamblers**
Poker & Other Casino Games

Published by
Huntington Press
3665 Procyon St.
Las Vegas, Nevada 89103
telephone: (702) 252-0655
facsimile: (702) 252-0675
email: books@huntingtonpress.com

Copyright © 2007, Jean Scott, Marissa Chien, EA

ISBN: 978-0-929712-53-6
$24.95us

Design & production: Laurie Shaw

**DISCLAIMER**
    The information presented in this book is intended as no more than a general guideline for the general public. Tax issues surrounding gambling can be extremely complicated and ultimately depends upon the "facts and circumstances" of each individual taxpayer. Although the authors and the publisher have made every effort to ensure the accuracy of this information, it's imperative that taxpaying gamblers consult with tax advisors regarding personal situation.

# Contents

# Foreword
## by Phil Gordon

When I met Marissa Chien about three years ago, my financial life was a mess. Like many professional gamblers, I had neglected many of my financial responsibilities. Being a "winner" makes that easy to do. The money just seems to roll in and there's always enough to cover whatever tournament buy-ins are required and whatever expenses are necessary.

I've been a professional poker player now for about eight years. Knock on wood, I've never had a losing year. Not everyone can run so good for so long. By my estimates, about 80% of the professional players you see on TV on a regular basis have been broke or are currently broke. It happens. This is a risky business. And at the end of the day, every dime you can save on taxes is a dime that mitigates your risk of going broke. It's "saving bets" that counts the most over the long term, not only in gambling, but also with the IRS.

Take my advice: Get on board with a solid accounting plan. You may not be able to use Marissa as your personal accountant like I'm fortunate enough to do. But you can use the solid information in this book, available nowhere else as far as I know, to stay square with the taxman, neither underpaying nor overpaying what you owe on your gambling winnings.

I used to absolutely dread April 15$^{th}$. Now it's just another day when I can go down to the casino and win some money and build my bankroll.

Best of luck, and may you be fortunate enough to have to pay some taxes on your gambling winnings year after year.

—Phil Gordon, poker professional

# Author's Notes

## JEAN SCOTT

This book started out to be a single chapter in my earlier book *More Frugal Gambling*. Due to my own experiences and the questions many casino players asked me, I knew that the tax implications of gambling were a big mystery to most people. So I began researching the subject. I read as many IRS publications as I could find and searched widely for tax information on the Internet. I talked to present and former IRS agents and to many tax preparers and accountants and lawyers.

I discovered that the IRS offers surprisingly few details to guide gamblers through the tax maze in which they find themselves. Furthermore, I found what the IRS does say is often general, vague, open to individual interpretation, and even contradictory. This may have been done intentionally, so that most gambling issues would fit under a large umbrella of general guidelines. Or, more likely, it's typical government bureaucracy that is slow to keep up with changing times.

Whatever the reason, it's difficult for an individual taxpayer to know exactly how to treat his particular gambling circumstances, and it has even ended up confusing the IRS itself. Therefore, you can't call one IRS phone number and get the final and absolute answer to your questions on gambling and federal income taxes—calling and talking to 10 different IRS representatives might give you up to 10 varying pieces of advice. Two auditors sitting next to each other in the same office could hear the same information and come up with entirely different results.

In addition, I quickly learned that many tax preparers aren't knowledgeable about gambling issues, even if they're experts in other tax areas. For many years before we moved to Las Vegas, I had to educate my otherwise-excellent accountants about gambling issues, though my own knowledge was extremely limited at the time.

However, when we moved to Vegas, Brad and I were fortunate to find a fellow gambler who was also a tax accountant—Marissa Chien. Finally, I had someone who, as a gambler as well as an Enrolled Agent, was knowledgeable about both gambling *and* taxes and could do our tax returns in such a way that we could be relatively certain that all the bases were covered accurately. Marissa gave me so much valuable input for my tax chapter, which she had kindly offered to edit, that I realized this was a much broader subject than I'd originally imagined.

A lightbulb came on in my head: I needed more of Marissa's input to cover this subject adequately, and it was definitely too much for one chapter in a book. It needed a whole book to itself, one that Marissa and I should write together. So that is how *Tax Help for Gamblers* was born.

We've retained most of the text of the original chapter, written in my folksy layman's style. Marissa went through it and added important information to explain some of the whys and hows of this complex subject, including tax-code specifics, relevant court cases, and professional comments. She also prepared the charts and forms in the section on state taxes and in the Appendix, to help readers better see the practical application of the information we cover.

Although the publisher has put a disclaimer in the front of this book, Marissa and I want to add some cautions here. I'm a teacher and a writer by profession, not an accountant or lawyer. Although I try to be clear in differentiating between facts and opinions, I want to emphasize that no one should base his or her actions solely on the information in this book. Even though Marissa is a qualified Enrolled Agent and has more technical knowledge in this area than I do, she strongly concurs. The information here is provided merely to help you become more knowledgeable about some of the thorny issues in this complex field.

Another caution: There are limitations with any tax information written in this (or any) book. Government tax policy is not a placid pond. It's an ever-changing river, with treacherous rapids along the way. Even professional tax preparers wage a constant battle to keep up to date on the changes; most individual taxpayers don't have a chance. Often, the first versions of commercial software you buy to help you do your own taxes have to be updated during the same tax season. This is the reason many knowledgeable and experienced do-it-yourself taxpayers still have a professional look over their returns just before they submit them to the government.

As always, we advise that you seek the advice of a tax professional to guide you in your *personal* tax decisions.

## MARISSA CHIEN

I'm a gambler myself. I owe a lot of what I know about video poker and maximizing my gambling dollar to the expertise of Jean Scott and her writing about smart gambling. Even with my specialization in taxes, when I tried to accurately report my gambling activities on my own tax returns, I began to realize that the laws relating to gambling are not very specific as they pertain to today's gambling environment. Even as a tax professional, I was finding it difficult to find clear guidance.

And if it was intricate for me, it's no surprise that the general public doesn't have a clue. Just from writing a couple of columns a year for the *Las Vegas Advisor* on the subject and preparing other gamblers' returns, not a week goes by that I don't get a call from someone from around the country asking for my help. No book out there deals with the nuances of gambling and tax returns completely enough to show how the IRS auditors look at this issue, and the IRS publications leave you with more questions than answers. With the proliferation of casinos—combined with the increased focus by the IRS on gamblers—this will become more of a problem for more taxpayers in the future.

Many people say, "I just give my tax preparer any paperwork I get from a casino and he/she takes care of all the details; I don't need to know all this stuff." The problem with this is that many of these tax professionals aren't gamblers themselves, thus aren't knowledgeable about the accompanying tax issues. So even though you don't do your own tax returns, you should have at least a basic knowledge of tax issues so that you're able to choose a knowledgeable tax preparer and provide enough records that he or she can do the best job.

# Part I

# Federal Taxes

*"If you want to make bets, your odds would be better to go to a casino."*

—Ex-IRS Commissioner Charles Rossotti, warning taxpayers just before the tax deadline in April 2001 not to be tempted by falling audit rates to cheat.

# 1
# The Basics

[Editor's Note: The writer alternates throughout the book between Jean and Marissa. When a change occurs, the writer is identified in the beginning of the first paragraph.]

**JEAN:** "Paying taxes on my gambling wins? You've got to be kidding. Sure, sometimes I win, but my losses are always much larger than my wins by the end of the year. So I don't have to mess with it on my federal or state tax returns."

Wrong! You probably should "mess with it," especially if you hold any of the following common, but *mistaken,* beliefs:

• I can lump together all my wins and losses for the year and, if I have a net loss, I don't need to put wins or losses on my income tax returns. After all, I didn't have any gambling income.

• The IRS can't "catch" me, even if I win a lot of money gambling, as long as it's done slowly over a considerable period of time in different gambling venues and I get no official forms like a W-2G or 1099.

- Federal and state tax agencies know most gamblers lose over the long term, so they aren't very interested in auditing them.
- If I do get a few W-2Gs, I can just count that total as my gambling income for the year and be safe in an IRS audit.
- If I gamble online, the IRS doesn't get any records of this, so I don't have to report any of my winnings.
- If I gamble on a cruise ship in waters three miles from U.S. soil, I don't need to report my winnings.
- If I play poker only in home games, I do not have to report my winnings.
- Winnings from illegal gambling are not taxable.

Before we go any further, let me emphasize: The purpose of this book is not to moralize about reporting or not reporting your gambling wins and losses. However, as casinos spring up around the country and, as a result, more and more people gamble, the IRS is becoming more interested in this area of potential under-reporting. If you report any W-2Gs, or don't include them when you've been issued them, it's becoming more likely you'll be asked by the IRS to provide more details of your gambling. And it's becoming more likely that you might be questioned about gambling if you come to the attention of the IRS for other reasons, even a routine audit.

**MARISSA:** However, you should also know that the IRS can't go on "fishing expeditions" if you're being audited. When the IRS audits you, they have to tell you specifically which area of your tax return they're examining. For example, if they're questioning the part of your return that shows you're claiming a room of your home for a business office, they must keep their investigation and questions to that one subject. However, if you open the door by commenting on other subjects, i.e., gambling, then they can question you about that area. (This is the reason it's usually best to have professionals speak for you at an audit—they know to stick carefully to the subject at hand. Taxpayers are often so nervous that they ramble all over the place in their effort to "explain.")

You should be aware that the Criminal Investigative Division (CID) of the IRS is beginning to investigate gamblers more thoroughly. The CID looks for people who willfully, with intent, try to defraud the IRS by under-reporting income or overstating losses and deductions. And they like to jump at the chance to leverage the publicity that they would get by making an example out of a gambler who is not properly reporting his gambling income.

Remember, not reporting income constitutes tax evasion and can have severe consequences. Just look at Richard Hatch, winner of the first TV "Survivor" show, who is in prison for skipping just one "little" detail on his tax return, his win of one million dollars!

**JEAN:** A Nevada note. On July 1, 2007, Nevada casinos, which for many years had been permitted to operate under the slightly different rules of state statue Regulation 6A, were required to switch to the Title 31 federal reporting rules that other states had been following for years. I discuss these new rules in Chapter 5 under the topic of "Big Brother is Watching You." The main difference that's bothering gamblers is that they're now asked for their Social Security numbers more often and for smaller amounts than $10,000. It's a catch-22 situation. You aren't required by law to give your SS number when buying in or cashing out for amounts that don't put you over the $10,000 report trigger for the day. However, the casinos are being more aggressive in asking for it anyway (so they won't accidentally run afoul of the new reporting rules and find themselves in a messy audit), and they may fill out that dreaded SAR (suspicious activity report) if you refuse to give it.

Supposedly, these stricter federal rules were forced on Nevada to stop money laundering by terrorists after 9/11, but some have speculated that it's really a way for the government to better track individual gambling action, so more taxes can be collected on previously unreported winnings.

> "May you get so many royal flushes that you'll have an income tax problem."
>
> —A wish for us from Jean's friend and Las Vegas e-newsletter publisher, Billhere.

## GAMING WINS AS INCOME

**JEAN:** IRS publications clearly state that gambling winnings are income and must be reported. The instruction booklets that come with tax forms list gambling winnings as one type of income to be put under "Other Income." One court case put it this way: "It is illegal not to report winnings, and you're risking possible prosecution for criminal tax evasion."

This means gambling winnings from legal, or even *illegal,* sources anywhere in the world: lotteries, raffles, drawings, prizes; racetracks; bingo games; and casino games, whether they're on Native American reservations, cruise ships, the Internet, or in another country. It means all gambling winnings, whether you get a W-2G, a 1099, or no paperwork at all.

**MARISSA:** Internal Revenue Code (IRC), section 61, states that *… gross income means all income from whatever source derived.* For example, if you sit down and play a penny slot machine for an hour, happen to win \$1, and walk away, you're technically required to report it on line 21, "Other Income," of Form 1040, even though there's no paper trail to your "income."

**JEAN:** Many people think they understand the gambling-income concept. "Hey, I'd be glad to report income for a year in which I actually won money gambling, but that hasn't happened yet." What they don't understand is that the IRS is not talking about one net win-or-loss figure at the end of the tax year, but win/loss figures for individual gambling sessions. They say: You cannot net out your gambling for the year. You must add up all the winning sessions and all the losing sessions separately. To emphasize this, the IRS puts

> "My tax-law professor in law school used to say (when asked if this or that was taxable), "If you find a penny on the street, it's taxable."
>
> —From Starr Piercy, Jean's attorney sister

this, in plain non-technical easy-to-understand language, in the instructions that come with your tax forms: *You cannot reduce your gambling winnings by your gambling losses and report the difference.*

**MARISSA:** In one famous court case in 1999, USA v. Scholl, a heavy gambler was found guilty of under-reporting his gambling income even though he was always a net loser at the end of the year. Those years he had a net loss he didn't report wins or losses. Years he got W-2Gs, he reported only that amount as his win.

The IRS must have information about both gambling income and gambling losses in order to determine whether income tax is owed. Whether Scholl believed (correctly or incorrectly) that he had lost more than he had won is irrelevant; the fact is that Scholl failed to report winnings and losses. "Whether there was an actual tax deficiency is irrelevant because the statute is a perjury statute." [See United States v. Marashi, 913 F.2d 724, 736 (9th Cir. 1990).]

Why was he accused of the more serious criminal offense of filing a false federal-income-tax return, rather than the less serious offense of violating tax laws? For one thing, he was a well-known Arizona Superior Court judge and the IRS loves to make examples of prominent taxpayers. However, another part of this case is that he was charged with "structuring"—that is, trying to circumvent the currency transaction reporting limits. He would make $5,000 cash deposits to different banks on the same day and not inform the banks involved. This is a federal offense. I'm just guessing here, but I think the IRS had a stronger case with the two pieces combined than if they had just one or the other. In any case, he was found guilty—but was sentenced to probation only.

Obviously, this is an extreme example. However, when you sign your return, the fine print says this is what you are doing: *Under penalty of perjury, I declare that I have examined the return and accompanying schedules and statements, and to the best of my knowledge and belief, that they are true, correct and complete.* And be assured that having someone else prepare your return does not relieve you of taking this final responsibility.

## ONLINE GAMBLING

**JEAN:** This is a good place to discuss online gaming. IRS regulations state that U.S. citizens and anyone who is considered a U.S. resident for tax purposes (i.e., resident aliens) must declare as income all gambling wins, from anywhere. IRC, Section 61, states that ... *gross income means all income from whatever source derived.* ... Although it isn't mentioned specifically, this includes cyberspace. It doesn't change just because online casinos don't issue W-2Gs or are headquartered in a country outside the U.S. Therefore, wise players do report wins/losses from online gaming, just as they do from bricks-and-mortar casinos. (However, I'm sure that many "forget" a lot of their wins and "remember" all their losses when April 15 comes around. Obviously, this is a common occurrence in any activity where no paperwork is sent to the IRS from the source of the income.)

This IRS requirement to report *all* income makes the question moot, at least in the taxation area, about whether online gambling is legal or not, no matter how long it takes for this to be decided by the U.S government, if it ever does become clear-cut. People earn money at more clearly defined illegal activities (i.e., prostitution, bookmaking, etc.) and do report that income—or at least some of it—on their tax returns.

In any case, if you have an online gambling account based in a foreign country with a balance of $10,000 or more at any time during the year, the Bank Secrecy Act requires you to report it to the IRS by filing a Report of Foreign Bank and Financial Accounts (FBAR). This is from the IRS website: *The FBAR is a tool to help the United States government identify persons who may be using foreign financial accounts to circumvent United States law. Investigators use FBARs to help identify or trace funds used for illicit purposes or to identify unreported income maintained or generated abroad.* To file the FBAR, you check the appropriate block on Schedule B of your 1040 tax return and file Form TD F 90-22.1, *Report of Foreign Bank and Financial Accounts,* with the Department of the Treasury (not the IRS).

**MARISSA:** I'm guessing that most people who earn income illegally aren't concerned about lawfully reporting it on a tax return. That's why criminals often get nailed. It's easier to convict someone for not filing a tax return than it is for drug dealing or prostitution. Remember, Al Capone was arrested and sentenced on tax evasion, which was easier to prove than the actual horrific crimes he committed.

**JEAN:** An aside here. The IRS end of the government is not supposed to share records with other government entities and the Supreme Court has previously ruled that the government can't use information on a tax return to prove an illegal activity.

**MARISSA:** Many gamblers have felt "safe" in not reporting their online wins, since online casinos, being headquartered in countries outside the U.S, do not issue any paperwork, like a W-2G, to the U.S. government. If I'd written this section a few years ago, I would have talked about the danger that the government in the future might decide to get records from credit-card companies and money-transfer businesses like SafePay, NETeller, and FirePay, to catch the past actions of online gamblers. This is what they did in 2000, obtaining MasterCard and American Express transactions billed to bank accounts in Antigua, Bermuda, the Bahamas, and the Cayman Islands to look for tax evaders using offshore accounts.

This is no longer a vague fear for online gamblers; it's already happening. Witness the ongoing investigation of NETeller. The U.S. Department of Justice now has complete information on everyone who has or ever had a NETeller account.

**JEAN:** You may wonder how things have changed since the surprising middle-of-the-night passage of the Unlawful Internet Gambling Enforcement Act of 2006 dealt a stunning blow to online gaming. Actually, it did not address the legality of online gaming, but knocked the legs out from under it, making it difficult for money-handlers to do business with American online players. Although a very few savvy online gamblers have found ways to get around these obstacles, the average U.S. online gambler has been stopped cold from betting with anything but play money.

Several bills in Congress are currently addressing this situation in different ways: by completely repealing the onerous (at least to gamblers) legislation passed last year, or by making online gaming legal but regulated, or by making poker an exception, because it's a game of skill rather than chance. And there's pressure from other countries that feel the U.S. is flouting international law.

Few want to predict how this will play out in the future. But no matter what's decided, I think I can safely say that the U.S government will always consider gambling wins as income, no matter from what source they come, and it will want these wins accounted for on a U.S. income tax return. I will even go out on a limb here, but probably a pretty safe one, and predict that there will be more government intervention in gambling matters in the future. And casinos, on land or sea or in cyberspace, will have to submit more, not fewer, records about player action.

## DEFINING A "WIN"

**JEAN:** OK, let's say you now understand that you must report all gambling income to the IRS and your wins are subject to taxes. The first question that may come to mind is, "What exactly is a gambling win?"

**MARISSA:** In my personal experience representing clients in audits, the IRS seems to define a gambling "win" as the net win one achieves in a particular session.

**JEAN:** "Okay," I hear you asking, "Just what is a session?"

Is it the few seconds during which you pulled the handle of a slot machine while waiting in line at the buffet and got back four more quarters than you put in? Is it a $10 win as you played one hand of blackjack with a coupon on the way to the restroom? Is it a $500 slot jackpot, although you already had lost $600 in the same machine that day? What about a $10,000 jackpot on a lucky trip to a riverboat near your home, which you took to Vegas the next week and blew it all, plus some more? Or three winning months of play in a casino wiped out completely by nine losing months that followed, giving you a net loss at the end of the year?

**MARISSA:** The problem is that nowhere in the entire tax code does the IRS use the word "session," much less specifically define it. IRS record-keeping guidelines speak about "specific wager or wagering activity." Obviously, a "specific wager" is the smallest unit of gambling time. But "wagering activity" is synonymous with "gambling session," and neither is specifically defined. There's no basic unit of accountability that will fit all gambling situations.

**JEAN:** But there's one key word that every gambler should understand and remember, and that's "records." What the IRS has to say about gambling record-keeping gives us a starting point in our quest for the answer to what a session is. We'll discuss this basic tax obligation in the next chapter.

# Taxes, The Law, and The Courts

Three different kinds of laws affect taxation in the U.S and we refer to all three of them throughout the book:

- The first is statutory tax law, which includes laws and treaties passed by Congress. This includes the Internal Revenue Code (IRC).
- The second is administrative tax law. This includes rules and regulations set down by the IRS, which is authorized by the IRC to administer the Code. Revenue Procedure 77-29 in Appendix C is an example of this.
- The third is judicial tax law, which is the body of court cases that have made decisions relating to income taxes since 1913, the year the Sixteenth Amendment gave Congress the power to collect income taxes.

John Walker, who developed the comprehensive website that contains the complete text of the Internal Revenue Code (www.fourmilab.ch/ustax/ustax), gives this important caution: "Please keep in mind that in the Anglo-Saxon legal system, the law is not so much what is written down, but what the courts have decided in cases. People, particularly folks with a background in engineering or science, often assume the law can be interpreted and manipulated like a set of axioms. It doesn't work that way. So while there is a great deal one can learn from a document such as the Internal Revenue Code, it's no substitute for expert professional advice when you're making decisions that affect your own wallet. Conversely, when dealing with experts, having access to the Code is a good way to find out just how expert they really are, and how accurate the advice you're getting actually is."

## Taxes, The Law, and The Courts *(cont'd.)*

Marissa and I have quoted some IRC text and referred to specific tax-court cases in both the body of this book and in the Appendix. But we urge you to use the above website when you have questions about tax law. We also recommend that you visit www.ustaxcourt.gov, an excellent source for the details of court cases on tax matters.

*"The Internal Revenue Code is about 10 times the size of the Bible—and unlike the Bible, contains no good news."*

—Don Rickles

# 2
# Player Record-Keeping

**MARISSA:** I'm sorry to report that the huge majority of gamblers do not keep any sort of record of their play. The truth is that a good gaming log is hard to keep up to date. When you finish gambling, you're often tired, maybe a bit bug-eyed, or even intoxicated. If you've won, you're on a high and want to celebrate, not write in a log. If you've lost, the last thing you want to do is record it for posterity. Perhaps, if you think about it at all, you figure that, whatever your result, you'll remember it if a time ever comes when you need to. Or you actually do write down your result—on a cocktail napkin that comes clean in the wash. Or you actually record your win or loss in a small spiral-bound pocket notebook, the kind reporters carry around, but you don't note enough details of your gambling session to appear authentic in any IRS audit.

Sure, keeping a log isn't easy. But trust me on this: It's easier than having to pay more in taxes than you're liable for, or worse, trying to justify a claim of gambling losses, without adequate documentation, to a steely-eyed bean-counting representative of the U.S. government.

# IRS GUIDELINES FOR RECORDS

**JEAN:** First, let me quote here from IRS publication 529, under the topic "Gambling Losses Up to the Amount of Gambling Winnings":

*Diary of winnings and losses. You must keep an accurate diary or similar record of your losses and winnings.*

*Your diary should contain at least the following information:*

- *The date and type of your specific wager or wagering activity.*
- *The name and address or location of the gambling establishment.*
- *The names of other persons present with you at the gambling establishment.*
- *The amount(s) you won or lost.*
- *Proof of winnings and losses.*

*In addition to your diary, you should also have other documentation. You can generally prove your winnings and losses through Form W-2G, Certain Gambling Winnings; Form 5754, Statement by Person(s) Receiving Gambling Winnings; wagering tickets, canceled checks, credit records, bank withdrawals, and statements of actual winnings or payment slips provided to you by the gambling establishment.*

*For specific wagering transactions, you can use the following items to support your winnings and losses:*

*__Keno__: Copies of the keno tickets you purchased that were validated by the gambling establishment, copies of your casino credit records, and copies of your casino check cashing records.*

*__Slot machines__: A record of the machine number and all winnings by date and time the machine was played.*

*__Table games__: Twenty-one [blackjack], craps, poker, baccarat, roulette, wheel of fortune, etc.: The number of the table at which you were playing.*

*Casino credit card data indicating whether the credit was issued in the pit or at the cashier's cage.*

**Bingo**: *A record of the number of games played, cost of tickets purchased, and amounts collected on winning tickets. Supplemental records include any receipts from the casino, parlor, etc.*

**Racing (horse, harness, dog, etc.)**: *A record of the races, amounts of wagers, amounts collected on winning tickets, and amounts lost on losing tickets. Supplemental records include unredeemed tickets and payment records from the racetrack.*

**Lotteries**: *A record of ticket purchases, dates, winnings, and losses.*

*Supplemental records include unredeemed tickets, payment slips, and winnings statements.*

Other supporting evidence to go with your diary, besides what's specifically mentioned in IRS guidelines, can be credit-card records, hotel receipts, airline tickets, casino markers—paperwork that shows you were actually in the place where your diary says you gambled on a particular day. I heard of one person who got a dated ATM receipt each day in a casino, although he didn't actually withdraw any money; this was his way of establishing supporting evidence, proof that he was where his diary said he was.

Be careful, however, that your supporting evidence isn't suspicious. In one tax case, the court threw out horserace betting tickets that were covered with heel marks!

**MARISSA:** I'd like to give you an additional resource to refer to on the subject of gambling record-keeping. Jean has quoted above from an IRS publication. These publications provide guidance and instruction to the taxpayer in preparing the tax return, usually in a more readable form than the actual text of governing laws. However, in Appendix C, we have printed the text of Revenue Procedure 77-29, which gives the actual law that lists what is needed to substantiate gambling wins and losses.

## DEFINING A "SESSION"

**MARISSA:** As we said in Chapter 1, the word "session" is not mentioned even once in the tax code, much less defined. So we have to depend on the shadowy technique of "reasonable interpretation."

One way to gain insight on how the IRS determines wins and losses is to see how they treat table players. You sit down at a blackjack table, for example, buy in for a specific amount of money, play for an hour or so, and leave. If you happen to win $500, that's noted by the pit personnel in your player file (if you've given them your name to be tracked). So to the IRS, that's also a gambling win. If you come back later that same day, sit down, play, and lose $500, to the IRS that's a gambling loss. They don't care what happens on a hand-by-hand basis. To them that's the equivalent of "churn" on a machine, that is, the coin-in and coin-out totals. This application of a gambling "session" was used in the case of Lutz v. Commissioner (2002), in which the court did not take into account casino slot-club printouts, but did use Trip History Reports that the casino had provided.

**JEAN:** The problem with IRS record-keeping guidelines is that they're merely implied parameters of a session, not an exact definition of a gambling time unit or the duration of a "wagering activity." It's fairly obvious in the example Marissa gives above what a "session" is. But what if you jump tables every few minutes, taking your chips with you, either sticking with blackjack or changing to another table game, such as roulette or craps, trying to find a "lucky" table where you can win? Even pit bosses often give up trying to track the wins and losses of a table-hopper.

The session concept seems similarly cut and dried for those who play the machines. If they play at one machine for an hour or more and quit for a while, that's their "session." But what if they're constantly moving all over a casino, carrying their coin cup—or now more likely their TITO (Ticket-In-Ticket-Out) slip—and playing a few hands on a number of slot machines, trying to find a "hot" one? What if they move from casino to casino playing all sorts of games, table and machine, for many very short periods over several days, dipping into the same original bankroll the whole time?

It's usually to the advantage of a taxpayer to have as long a session as possible in order to have the lowest gross total for winning sessions; we discuss the compelling reasons for this in later chapters. However, what a person counts as a gambling session, in the absence of clear-cut instructions, has to be based on consistency, reasonableness, and practicality, depending on the circumstances in each individual case. One tax expert put it this way: "My advice is to use whatever definition you feel that you could defend in an IRS audit with a straight face and without sweating."

Many casual recreational gamblers count, for example, a three-day trip to Vegas as one long gambling session, during which they play at many different machines and tables. Many lose all track of time and there are no time divisions like a day, much less a session, as they gamble off and on the whole time, with just occasional short snatches of sleep. When they get home, they may summarize in a diary the various games they played and the casinos they played in, but with no minute-to-minute details, just a win or loss figure at the end of this one long marathon gambling session. At the end of the year, they correctly add all their winning trips for a total win figure and all their losing trips as the total loss and put those two figures in the appropriate places on their tax return.

**MARISSA:** I'd have to advise someone that using a multi-day trip as a session is usually too long a time frame. I would find this hard to defend to an IRS auditor. In my experience, they want a session to be more discrete than this. However, there might be logical exceptions, especially for someone in a tournament situation. Poker or blackjack tournaments may run over several days with one result at the end of the tournament.

**JEAN:** Many people, especially those who gamble often, define a gambling session as one day. They cite the phrase "the date" from the list of things Revenue Procedure 77-29 says you should put in your diary. So they note the daily total in either the win or loss column of their logs. Some people are even more detailed, counting it a new session if they change games during the day—e.g., from video poker to blackjack—or if they move to another casino to play the same game. They cite the same list that talks in the singular about a "specific wager" and a "wagering activity."

Here's how one astute Internet friend put it when asked how he would justify the "daily-session" method if he were audited: "I would tell them that many of the data elements are simply not appropriate to track on a micro level. Some days are composed of lots of jumping around between machines/tables/etc. It works best to take an accounting at the end of each day as a total of all activities, much like a business does when counting the register and recording total cash activity for the day."

**MARISSA:** One point I want to mention here is that having no records is better than having fabricated records. Provisions within the IRS code allow for estimated tax returns. Let's say that you didn't keep any records during the year. Under the tax code, you're allowed to file a tax return using estimated amounts for income and losses. Should you go this route, you would need to attach a statement explaining very clearly how you came up with your numbers and why your method is appropriate. This method of filing a tax return is definitely not for the faint of heart and should not be tried without professional assistance. The worst thing you can do is make something up or not disclose that you used estimated numbers. Now you're liable for penalties, including criminal ones.

**JEAN:** Whatever you decide a gambling session is for you and whatever kind of record-keeping system you set up, the IRS is very clear on one concept. It's in the tax instructions, in plain language, with no ambiguity: Your records should show your winnings separately from your losses. In other words, you cannot net out the totals at the end of the year.

However, for the rest of the details, your best course of action is to try to follow the *intent* of the guidelines with *reasonable* interpretation and implementation. Even in the more formal writing of Revenue Procedure 77-29, there are many qualifying words: *An accurate diary or similar record regularly maintained by the taxpayer, supplemented by verifiable documentation will usually be acceptable evidence for substantiation of wagering winnings and losses. In general, the diary should contain at least the following information* ... Notice the words "usually" and "In general," which don't appear in the IRS tax-instruction booklets.

The IRS doesn't believe that one size fits all. Revenue Procedure 77-29 ends like this: *The record-keeping suggestions set forth (in this ruling) are intended as general guidelines to assist taxpayers in establishing their reportable gambling gains and deductible gambling losses. While following these will enable most taxpayers to meet their obligations under the Internal Revenue Code, these guidelines cannot be all inclusive and the tax liability of each depends on the facts and circumstances of particular situations.*

One final note on your gambling record-keeping: You *do not* need to send your log with your tax return. The same thing is true for all those supplemental receipts you collected and win-loss statements. It also includes W-2Gs you received from casinos, unless there were withholding amounts. Just put them all together in a safe place and hope you never have to get them out again. But in two or three years, if you read or hear those dreaded words, "You are being audited," you'll be glad you have all these records to back up the figures you put on your tax return.

How long do you need to keep these records? Revenue Procedure 77-29 addresses this question: *Under Section 6001 of the Code, taxpayers must keep records necessary to verify items reported on their income tax returns. Records supporting items on a tax return should be retained until the statute of limitation on that return expires.* That is three years under normal circumstances and six years if there's a gross understatement (over 20%) of income or tax liability. However, there is no limitation to how far the IRS can go back if they can prove fraud.

> Keeping a gambling log because the IRS requires it isn't the only reason for a wise gambler to do so. Maintaining a consistent and accurate record of your wins and losses sobers you to the real costs of gambling. You have visible evidence—right there on the page in stark black and red—of your cumulative result. If you're in the black, you're doing something right (or you got lucky). If you're in the red, your diary might indicate to you that you're losing more than you want to or should, in which case you can adjust your approach.

## CASINO WIN/LOSS STATEMENTS

**JEAN:** Some people feel they can skip having a diary if they get win/loss statements from casinos at the end of the year. These are valuable as supporting evidence of play, but many tax-court decisions have upheld the IRS position that they don't substitute for a gambling log. For one thing, in the case of machine play, they cover only the time you played with your slot club card inserted. Many people don't ever use a card or use it only sporadically. In the case of table play, you'd have needed to give your name to the pit boss and ask to be rated (something many players don't do) for the casino to keep any records at all of your wins and losses; in addition, these are only human estimates (and will remain so until table games are computerized, something that's already being done in a few places and will become more common within a few years).

Furthermore, casino win/loss statements vary greatly in accuracy and completeness, because there's no standard form for the casino to use. Some forms for machine players are quite detailed if the casino has a good computer-tracking system, giving the exact time and win/loss figure for each day of the year you played a machine with your slot club card at their casino. Others merely give a total yearly win/loss figure, and sometimes this is only an estimate based on theoretical machine hold, rather than your actual wins or losses. Still others may give you your lifetime total, rather than just one for the past year. Many statements are notoriously inaccurate and incomplete, often not counting hand-pays and/or W-2G jackpots, but not making that fact known. A few we get match our own records fairly closely; most seem to have little relationship to our own extremely detailed records.

To get one of these win/loss statements, you need to ask at the players club, either in person or by phone. Some casino websites let you make the request online. Sometimes the casino asks that you make the request in writing; some issue printed forms for you to fill out. Occasionally, you might be required to have the request notarized. In any case, although they're useful as supplemental information, you shouldn't depend on them as your only records. They may be good for proof that you played at a certain casino on a certain day, but not as evidence to support a loss deduction.

**MARISSA:** The biggest problem with casino win/loss statements is all of the disclaimer language that they put at the bottom of the statements. In a Tax Court Memorandum, Mayer v. Commissioner (2000), the court gave no probative value to the win/loss statements that the taxpayer produced, because of the disclaimer at the bottom. I can see the issue from both sides. I think the casinos don't want to stick their necks out on any issue if they don't have to, but it's also difficult for a casino to produce an accurate win/loss statement anyway, since it has no assurance or proof that a gambler uses his/her card all the time. The IRS will consider it supporting evidence only. The win/loss statements in and of themselves will usually not get you through an audit.

However, there's a real danger I must warn you about in using casino win/loss statements, particularly those that give coin-in and coin-out figures. They can end up biting you in the butt. On the one hand, they can get a taxpayer off the hook for not having good records, but then it creates other problems. Right now, there is a general trend within the IRS to accept these statements, but then they use your *gross* coin-out as your win figure, a *much* bigger one than your session total win would be if you kept good records.

In Chapter 4 we talk at length about the financial disaster a large gross-gaming-win figure can bring, because of the increase to your AGI (Adjusted Gross Income). This isn't a problem just on the federal return, but on many state returns as well. People in states that don't allow gaming losses to be deducted on state returns may be hit with unbelievable tax bills, because of high gross gambling wins, even if they use session-win figures.

When the IRS and/or the state (or even an uninformed tax preparer who isn't familiar with gambling issues) decide to use the win/loss statements, some real horror stories have emerged. Using coin-out figures is counting every hand on a video poker machine or every pull on a slot machine as a "session," even those that result in a push (meaning a tie, or winning the same amount as your bet). Obviously, that's not a reasonable stance. It would be like counting every hand at a blackjack table or every spin of the roulette wheel.

But it has caused many taxpayers to have high tax bills, or to have to go to extreme efforts to fight one. Since it doesn't pay to give the government any more information than necessary, I recommend that you keep good records yourself. Then you won't need to show auditors your win/loss statements.

There *is* something you can get from the casinos, if you need supplemental proof at an audit. You can request "trip histories." I've heard of one top tax lawyer who won his point in tax court by getting letters from the general counsels of the casinos, which included information that wasn't on the win/loss statements. Revenue Procedure 77-29 supports such a maneuver: *Additional supporting evidence could also include affidavits or testimony from responsible gambling officials regarding wagering activity.*

# THE GAMING LOG

**JEAN:** The IRS demands that you keep a gambling diary or "similar record," but doesn't give any details about what this diary should look like. Should it be a simple little notebook or pocket calendar you carry with you, in which you jot down details in real time after every session? Or can you go to a computer after each session and input all the details into an elaborate spreadsheet? I've known people who've done it both ways and the IRS accepted their records. And with the advent of small personal electronic devices, many players just directly enter the info directly into them when they finish a session, thereby bypassing the step of having to transfer info from paper to computer.

**MARISSA:** IRS publications and regulations do give some details about what information you should/can put in your diary, as Jean quoted from Publication 529 at the beginning of this chapter or is listed in Revenue Procedure 77-29 (which you can read in its entirety in Appendix C). These are general and may not fit all gambling endeavors, but it's a start to help us know what to put in our logs:

1. date and game or type of gambling;
2. name of place where you are gambling;
3. address where gambling takes place;
4. name of people (if any) with you when you are gambling;
5. amount you won or lost.

No guidelines are given for what you "must" put in your log for particular games, but we can get some ideas from the list of "supporting documentation" for specific games. Earlier, we talked about a "session" and decided that it would be unreasonable to expect someone to keep track of every hand at a casino **table game** or on a **machine**. Therefore, a session for those games might be a daily total, or you would have a session total when you changed tables/machines or went to a new game. For **race betting**, however, a court case ruled that you cannot lump together all the races in one meet for a net win or loss figure. You must record your win or loss for *each* race or proposition bet. **Sports betting** isn't mentioned in Revenue Procedure 77-29, but logical extrapolation would dictate that **sports betting** does follow race-betting rules. For **lottery** play, 77-29 seems to imply that you use the same rules as for race betting: Each ticket is a separate win or loss, although it might be logical to lump tickets together if they were all for one game.

For **bingo,** it seems permissible to lump together all your games in one bingo session and have one win or loss figure for your log. The guidelines for **keno** aren't clear, because they don't differentiate between paper and machine keno. If you consider the time element, paper keno is more like bingo or race betting and could be treated similarly. Machine keno is fast, so you might put them in your log the same way as for video poker or slot machines.

However, some of these more specific suggestions for individual games just don't seem to fit certain types or styles of gambling, especially the kind done in a modern-day casino. As an example, they mention putting machine numbers in your diary if you play slots. This is easy enough to do if you play one machine for a long length of time; however, this would be unworkable for someone who frequently jumps from machine to machine. The record-keeping would take more time than the actual gambling activity. (Actually, this isn't a bad idea. The less time your money is at risk in a game where the casino has the edge, the less money you will lose in the long term.)

**JEAN:** Actually, it's easier to talk about what kind of a diary the IRS is not likely to accept—one that's cobbled together at the end of the year, based on memory. I've heard stories of people who hit a big jackpot at the end of the year, then decided to create a whole-year diary at that time, with enough losing sessions so they could write off the win. This is very difficult to make believable—and some have been stopped in their tracks during an audit, because the early losses they fabricated were more than their total income during that period!

Out of one tax case came this official ruling: *Entries to your diary or log must be made when the gambling activity takes place. Your records may be determined to be inadequate if a handwriting expert testifies many of the entries were made at the same time.*

## HOW JEAN KEEPS RECORDS

Because I'm a details person (and perhaps because I'm a little paranoid), I try to cover all the bases. Before I had a computer, I kept detailed daily pocket-calendar records. When I got a computer, I was so proud of my ability to make a spreadsheet that I kept only these records for the first year, trying to update them after each gambling day. However, I found that I sometimes forgot to input the details for a couple of days. Then Brad and I had to wrack our brains to remember them, a harder job as we got older.

I also learned that the IRS likes real-time records. So now I carry a calendar notebook (see Figure A on page 28) with me when I go into a casino and jot down the details immediately after I finish playing. Then every few days I transfer the information to my computer spreadsheets (see Figure B on page 28). Since we may play more than one type of game in more than one casino in one day, we often have several session figures per day. I figure the more detailed my records, the happier the IRS will be.

## Figure A

**NOVEMBER '03**

**10 MONDAY** — HARRAHS - VEGAS

7/1 Harrah's - $1 JoB TP
+ 2080 - $30 Tips = + $2050
W2G - B - $4000
4/4 NYNY - Qrt NSUD 5P - $555
HR - Slot Coupon + 10

**11 TUESDAY** HARRAH'S - VEGAS
Veterans Day / Remembrance Day (Canada)

2/2 HARRAH'S - $1 JoB TP
                     - $2200

4/4 Gold Coast - Qrt NSUD MS
    "     "     CB +220 | +150

**12 WEDNESDAY**

Terribles - BJ
           MATCH
           PLAY
              - $25

TUNICA - GOLD STRIKE **THURSDAY 13**

7/1 Craps    + $105
2/2 BJ       - 60

TUNICA - GOLD **FRIDAY 14**
         STRIKE

BJ MATCH PLAY
           + $5

**SATURDAY 15**
PALMS
# $100 2-team parlay sports bet
  - 100

**SUNDAY 16**
Palms : $110 sports bet +100
2/2 Qrt FPDW Prog - +200

"Speech is silver; silence is golden."
— German Proverb

## Figure B

| | A | B | C | D | E | F | G | H | I | J | K |
|---|---|---|---|---|---|---|---|---|---|---|---|
| 1 | | | | GAMBLING | LOG | | LOW ROLLERS | | 2003 | | |
| 2 | | | | | | | | | | | |
| 3 | | | | | | | | | | | |
| 4 | Date | Hotel | Casino | Game | B-Hrs | J-Hrs | Notes | WIN | LOSS | W2G's - B | W2G's - J |
| 5 | | | | | | | | | | | |
| 6 | Nov. 10 | Harrahs | Harrahs | $1 JoB TP | 1 | 1 | | $2,050 | | $4,000 | |
| 7 | | | NYNY | Qrt NSUD 5P | 4 | 4 | | | 555 | | |
| 8 | | | Hard R | Slot Coupon | | | | $10 | | | |
| 9 | Nov. 11 | Harrahs | Harrahs | $1 JoB TP | 2 | 2 | | | 2200 | | |
| 10 | | | Gold C | Qrt NSUD MS | 4 | 4 | | 150 | | | |
| 11 | | | | Cashback | | | | 220 | | | |
| 12 | Nov. 12 | | Terribles | BJ Match Play | | | | | $25 | | |
| 13 | Nov. 13 | Gold S | Gold Strk | Craps | 1 | 1 | Tunica | 105 | | | |
| 14 | | | | BJ | 2 | 2 | | | 60 | | |
| 15 | Nov. 14 | Gold S | Gold Sirk | BJ Match Play | | | Tunica | $5 | | | |
| 16 | Nov. 15 | | Palms | $100 Parlay | | | 2-team | | 100 | | |
| 17 | Nov. 16 | | Palms | $110 Sports Bet | | | 1-team | 100 | | | |
| 18 | | | | Qrt FPDW Prog | 2 | | | 200 | | | |

# On Keeping a Tax Diary

A friend of Jean's, Anteroz, posted on an Internet forum this very practical advice. "I would like to preface my remarks by disclosing that for almost 15 years, I was called to testify in many cases as a drug expert where I would refer to notes made at the time of the analysis in the laboratory. In addition, I did send my entire tax diary to the IRS in 1995 as part of an audit.

"In general, I always make entries in ink in a bound booklet. If I make a mistake, I do not tear out the sequentially numbered page, but merely mark through the error and continue on. I make my entries while in action and therefore the entries are in various shades of blue or black ink. Sometimes tell-tale water marks from drinks are also visible. My handwriting varies from very neat to a scribble format. Just like a news reporter scribbling notes, your diary should look like you are in the field.

"When I get home, using a spreadsheet, I summarize by day and by game, my win/loss figures. The raw data from your accompanying notebook is what gives credibility to your computer printouts."

*"The best things in life are free, but sooner or later the government will find a way to tax them."*

—Anonymous

# 3
# Special Gaming Situations

## CASINO COMPS AND GIFTS

**JEAN:** Not all activity in a casino results in a clear-cut win-or-loss dollar figure. What about the T-shirt you get as a free gift when joining a casino players club? What about comps—meals, hotel rooms, show tickets—that the casinos give players to reward them for, and to try to keep, their loyalty? These areas aren't directly addressed in IRS publications, but most tax experts have concluded, from past IRS cases, that these kinds of comps do not need to be declared as gambling income and the casinos have not been instructed to issue 1099s for them.

However, often a casino does give 1099s for more major gifts to customers—e.g., cars to the highest-rolling whales—and the IRS has ruled that the fair-market value of these has to be included in gambling income, but can be offset by gambling losses. Brad and I were awarded a free cruise by one casino in a promotion based on machine play. We thought it would be considered a comp, just like the free rooms, food, and other benefits we'd received from this casino in the past, comps we'd "earned." However, we were issued a 1099 and Marissa said we'd have to count the fair market value of the cruise in our gambling income on our tax return.

The subject of comps is a huge gray area and there's no uniformity of casino policy when it comes to issuing 1099s. Also, there's no standardized interpretation of this issue by various tax preparers or even by IRS employees.

## CASHBACK AND FREE PLAY

**JEAN:** Related to comps, in that the casino often uses it to reward their players club members, cashback is a popular gambler benefit about which the IRS has yet to make a ruling, and again there's no consensus on how to treat it, even among tax experts. Casinos usually don't issue 1099s for cashback, even if you collect a large amount at one time, though a very few casinos do issue a 1099 if it's more than $600, treating it as a prize, or they'll give a W-2G if more than $1,200, treating it as a machine jackpot.

And to confuse matters, some casinos give you a choice of cash or comps for the points you earn in their players club. Thus, many players believe that cashback falls under the same category as comps, a reward from the casino that's not gambling income. Others feel it's more like a rebate of some of your losses and should reduce the total losses that you report. This is another gray area and you need to discuss your particular situation with your tax preparer.

**MARISSA:** I tell my clients that cashback is gambling income, whereas free buffets aren't. The standard I apply is that cashback is statutory, while a comp from the slot club booth or your host, such as the free buffet, is discretionary. Since the comp is entirely up to the host's discretion—i.e., he or she could refuse to issue it for any reason—to me that doesn't fall under the definitions of income under the tax code. Cashback is earned pursuant to a particular formula, and you're entitled to that cashback if you meet the statutory requirements of earning it.

The biggest argument as to why cashback is income is that if you're 86ed (barred) from a Nevada casino, Nevada Gaming Control has ruled time and time again that you're entitled to the cashback earned, whereas comps in your comp account are forfeited, since they're discretionary.

**JEAN:** These days casinos often give you free play instead of cash rewards. Free play is machine credits that must be played through a video poker or slot machine at least once before you can cash it out for money that you can put in your pocket. Here, again, we have a gray area that is not specifically addressed by the IRS or any court cases. Some people don't include free play in their gambling win, since they say it's just like comps, a non-cash gift from the casino. Some only count as a win what they actually have left to cash out after they play it through the machine once, as required by the casino. Others keep churning it through the machine until they have nothing left (in which case they feel they have no "win") or until they hit a big jackpot (which they do count as a win).

**MARISSA:** I recommend that free play be incorporated into one's log of session results. If someone receives $2,500 in free play, they should report the actual proceeds after playing it through the machine as a win. A big difference between free play and cashback is the fact that free play always has an expiration date and is usually valid for only a short period of time. Cashback can expire as well (for example, if for a lack of play during a set period your players account is closed), but it's usually available to collect for a much longer period of time.

**JEAN:** Here's another nuance of the cashback issue. I feel that cashback should be reported as income when you earn it and it's available to you, even if you don't collect it until a later time. Others may disagree, pointing out that there might be valid reasons for not collecting cashback, as when it's a small amount or a player plans to pick it up later, but doesn't get back to that casino before his account is closed.

Free play is a different situation. Many players, myself included, don't always collect their free play, especially if it's a small amount and/or it's not convenient or a good use of one's time to go back to that casino before it expires. Therefore, it's logical not to count it as gambling income until you actually redeem it.

**MARISSA:** The difference between cashback and free play involves the concept of "constructive receipt." It's like getting interest in a savings account. When the bank gives you interest, it counts it as income, even though you don't spend it or withdraw it from your bank account. But the money is yours with no restrictions for you to withdraw at anytime. Free play is just that: credits on a machine that you can use to play. In order for the money to be "yours," you have to run it through the machine at least once. Once it's been run through, now you have control over the funds; in other words, you now have constructive receipt. You can cash out or continue playing.

## CASINO TOURNAMENTS AND DRAWINGS

**JEAN:** The IRS treats all prizes and awards as income and this includes those won in a casino tournament or drawing. Awards and prizes given in goods or services must be counted as well as cash.

Those IRS rules seem clear enough, and sometimes casino tournaments and drawing prizes are treated just like non-gambling ones. For example, if your casino prize is a non-cash item, you can include it in your income at its fair market value. The "real" value of most prizes is usually much lower than what tax accountants often call the "fictitious value."

For example, when I won a car in a drawing at the Stardust some years ago, I had to pay taxes only on the amount I got when I sold it back to the dealer, a lower amount than the sticker price listed on the 1099 form the casino gave me. In the case of the cruise we won, described above under "Comps," the casino put the "brochure price" on the 1099 issued, an inflated amount that no one ever has to pay. We attached a copy of a listing on the Internet that showed the same cruise at a much-reduced price and put down that amount as the fair market value.

**MARISSA:** If you happen to win a non-cash prize in a casino drawing, you can definitely report the fair market value of that prize, even if it's less than the amount reported to you on a 1099-MISC. But you need to attach a note to your tax return explaining why the amount you're reporting is less than the amount shown on the 1099. Otherwise, a computer might kick out this discrepancy and trigger a letter from the IRS questioning you about this "undeclared income." To support the figure you give for the fair market value, I tell my clients to save things like newspaper ads or copies of Internet catalog pages indicating the price for which you could have bought the prize. These aren't attached to the original return, but are useful for a possible future audit.

**JEAN:** Even though some of the IRS general rules and instructions for prizes will be helpful to gamblers, many issues with the tax treatment of casino tournaments and drawings are perplexing.

First, let's talk about tournaments. The IRS has ruled that a tournament prize must be counted as income without subtracting the tournament fee. I once had to count a $600 tournament prize as a "win," even though I paid $1,000 to enter the darn thing. Players can add the tournament fees to their losses if they itemize and list gambling losses as a deduction. But often they reach the allowable loss amount before deducting the entry fees, thus they end up paying taxes on the gross win amount and it becomes the "prize that cost me money."

Poker tournaments have even more complicated rules set by the IRS, and we discuss these in Chapter 6.

The next puzzler for gambling taxpayers is what I call the "battle of the forms." It's standard that winners of non-gambling prizes will be issued Form 1099-MISC for prizes worth $600 or more. But much isn't "standard" when you're talking about the policies of various casino companies.

Many casinos do issue a 1099 for tournament prizes. However, some casinos issue that form for a win of $600 or more in *one* tournament, while others add all the tournament wins of any amount for one person in one year and issue a 1099 for the aggregate prizes that total $600 or above. And to complicate matters, some casinos issue a W-2G instead of a 1099.

For drawings, casinos usually follow the general rules for all prizes, just as non-gaming companies would. They issue a 1099 for prizes they value at $600 or more. Only on a rare occasion might a casino issue a W-2G for a drawing prize. In fact, one Las Vegas locals casino obtained a determination from the gaming specialist at the local IRS office in Las Vegas to use a W-2G instead of a 1099 for drawing prizes. (Yes, there actually is a position called gaming specialist here in the Las Vegas IRS office.)

Why is it important to gamblers whether a casino issues a W-2G or a 1099 for tournament and drawing prizes?

The question is whether gamblers can add casino drawing prizes and tournament wins to their "regular" casino wins. This isn't clearly stated by the IRS, but most gamblers put them in their log, just as they do all their gambling wins, no matter what form the casino issued. And most tax preparers recommend that you lump them all together in your total gross win *if* they're directly related to gambling. One tax preparer, when asked if the nature of the casino paperwork determined how to report something, responded: "The character of the income is not changed by the form on which the casino reports it—the 1099 or the W-2G."

It seems not to be a problem with the IRS if a tournament or drawing prize amount appears on a W-2G. That's understandable, since the name of the W-2G form is "Certain Gambling Winnings." However, I recently received some reports of people having trouble convincing unknowledgeable IRS personnel that casino tournament or drawing wins on which a 1099 is issued are gambling related and could/should be added into their gross win total.

**MARISSA:** In my experience thus far, if you include gambling-related 1099s in with your gambling winnings, it usually doesn't result in a query from the IRS. If it does, a letter of explanation usually clears up the matter.

Let's say you won a big-screen TV in a drawing where you had to earn tickets by gambling. The value of that TV was reported to you on a 1099-MISC. Since you won that prize through the direct act of gambling, it's technically gambling income. The same logic applies to invited-guest tournaments and events as it does to drawings. If previous gambling is a criterion for the invite and you're expected and even required, albeit tacitly, to gamble to receive future invitations, then the winnings from these tournaments and drawings should be considered gambling income, not prizes.

On the other hand, if you win a car on "The Price is Right," that's not gambling income. You'll still put the value of that prize under "Other Income" on your tax return, but on a separate line than your gambling wins. And, unfortunately, this amount cannot be offset by gambling losses.

Most tax employees in the Ogden Service Center (which services Las Vegas) are more knowledgeable about gaming issues than in other districts in the U.S. and, for the last few years, haven't questioned the returns of gamblers who lumped together totals from 1099s and W-2Gs, even if they didn't add a detailed list of each one. However, I always recommend that you include this list and, for possible extra security from IRS problems, you might add a notation that all your 1099 wins came from gambling-related activity.

**JEAN:** This all becomes an important issue if you itemize on Schedule A. If all kinds of gambling wins are lumped together, then perhaps you'll be able to offset some (or all) of your drawing and tournament wins by taking your gambling losses as a deduction, up to the amount of your wins. Again, you need to talk to a professional tax preparer who can analyze the details of your personal situation. But a great idea is to keep tournament and drawing literature that spells out how they are connected to your regular gambling. This could be powerful supporting evidence if you're ever audited.

**MARISSA:** Recently, a new wrinkle has appeared. Some casinos are starting to charge a token amount (perhaps only $1) for their formerly free invitational tournaments, so they feel that they can now report the prizes on a W-2G instead of a 1099. This is a trend I love. It would make it so much easier for gambling taxpayers if casinos could use the W-2G for any kind of wins connected with gambling.

**JEAN:** There's also another recent sign that's encouraging. For the first time, a government entity, the U.S. Tax Court, has chimed in on this Battle of the Forms. In the gambling case TSCHETSCHOT v. Commissioner (Feb. 2007), this footnote appeared: "… a casino's decision to issue a Form W2-G, *Certain Gambling Winnings*, or a Form 1099-Misc., *Miscellaneous Income*, does not affect the nature of the winnings for tax purposes."

Unfortunately, this specific case cannot be cited as precedent, because the court issued what's called a tax-court memorandum and this case doesn't make it to the level of a "full" case. Also, the quote is an ancillary comment by the court (actually a footnote in the document). The primary case was about an entirely different gambling matter than the 1099 versus W-2G issue. However, it would certainly be a talking point in dealing with the IRS at the administrative levels.

## GAMBLING GROUPS

**JEAN:** Gambling groups can range from informal partnerships between two friends who decide to pool their bankrolls in order to reduce individual risk in playing at higher levels to large highly organized teams, such as blackjack or progressive-machine players and syndicates that organize for large gambling endeavors. IRS form 5754, *Statement by Person(s) Receiving Gambling Winnings*, can be used for these group arrangements. (See sample form and instructions in Appendix A3.) This allows the casino to issue W-2Gs to each member of the group for his part in the win, rather than the one winner getting a W-2G for the total amount.

**MARISSA:** The person who actually wins the tournament or jackpot fills out Form 5754 with the names and Social Security numbers of any person(s) who shares in this win and gives it to the casino, which is required to accept this form and issue individual W-2Gs based on the information furnished on it. But here's where it can get tricky. I've found that many casino employees, especially those who pay off machine jackpots, are either unknowledgeable about this form or are unwilling to bother with it. A player could insist, but most won't, because of negative consequences.

For example, if you're using someone else's players card, the casino could be forced to recognize the 5754 if the jackpot is really someone else's. Perhaps you're playing with their money and you don't want the tax consequences of a jackpot. But then the casino would probably revoke both your players card accounts, since casinos frown on people playing on a card that is not their own. And the last thing you want the casino to think is that you're a member of a "team." Most casinos will 86 any player they think is on an organized team, because they categorize team players as "skillful" (and they're right in this opinion!).

Therefore, Form 5754 is rarely used, even in poker tournaments, the only place where players teaming up is a common and accepted custom.

However, there's a simple alternative: The one W-2G jackpot winner issues 1099s to each of the partners for the agreed-upon share. In all partnering cases, a written agreement signed up front by the partners is desirable.

**JEAN:** More complicated group options include forming a partnership, corporation, or limited liability company (LLC) and filing the special tax forms these require. These entities can be complex to set up and administer and usually require professional assistance. Therefore, they often cost more for most gamblers than their advantage would add, unless it's a large operation.

**MARISSA:** Reporting gambling winnings, especially from slot jackpots, within an entity is definitely an untested area of the tax code. Jennings v. Commissioner has allowed gambling income that's earned through a partnership and reported on a K-1 to maintain a gambling-income character, thereby allowing gambling losses to be deducted against it. Whether or not a similar situation with the use of corporations or LLCs is valid has not been ruled upon by the IRS.

---

In June 2006, Brad and I had a casino experience that gave me a lot of real-life examples for subjects in this chapter. We'd been in more than a hundred tournaments in the 21 years we'd been playing in casinos, many little ones and quite a few big ones. But Brad, because of his heavy play in the past, was invited to the biggest slot tournament that Caesars in Vegas had ever had before and certainly the biggest one we'd ever been in. There was a million-dollar total prize package, with first prize paying $500,000.

Well, to make a long story short, Brad was hot on the tournament machines in all four sessions and came out on top, snagging that amazing half-million!

To understand what I learned from this experience, some background information is needed. First, this tournament required a $10,000 entry fee. But you could get that refunded if you put in a certain amount of play on the floor outside the tournament times. The amount of that play was huge and required a bigger bankroll than we wished to risk. It also involved more hours per day than we wished to play. You were permitted to choose another person to be your partner, so we made a deal with our best friends that the two couples would share the monetary risk and playing time and then split any tournament winnings.

So there were two deliriously happy couples that night when the first-place winner was announced.

When we all finally settled down, next came the business details. First, Brad asked tournament officials if we could split the payoff with the other couple by using a Form 5754. However, their refusal didn't surprise us, because we remembered reading this notice on the official rules: "If you are playing as a team, your team member's name must be listed. All monies won will be payable to the main player. It is the responsibility of that player to distribute winnings to their partner. Main player is responsible for all applicable taxes."

That was certainly clear. So Brad accepted the check for $500,000.

The next surprise was the form that came with the check. It was a W-2G instead of the 1099 we expected. That was good. There was no doubt that this win would be gambling income, but the W-2G solidified that stance.

"Wait!" you might interrupt here. "You and Brad weren't going to pay taxes on the whole $500,000, were you?"

No, we gave our friends a check for $250,000 *and* a 1099 for that amount. We each added $250,000 to our other gambling wins for the year and put that total on our own income-tax returns.

From this exciting experience, I also got some real-life material for the next chapter, since we were all glad we file as professional gamblers and could shelter some of this win in retirement accounts.

*"We have long had death and taxes as the two standards of inevitability. But there are those who believe that death is the preferable of the two. 'At least,' as one man said, 'there's one advantage about death; it doesn't get worse every time Congress meets.'"*

—Erwin N. Griswold

# 4
# Filing Your Tax Return

**JEAN:** Okay, you've kept your gambling diary faithfully all year long. You've added up all your wins for the year to get one total and added up all losses for another total. Now, how do you put this information on your tax return?

This depends on whether you're a recreational gambler—as most gamblers are—or can file as a professional gambler (the latter having been firmly established as a recognized option by the courts only within the last generation).

## THE RECREATIONAL GAMBLER

**JEAN:** Casual or recreational gamblers can usually handle fairly easily the job of recording their gross gambling wins on their tax returns. You must use the long Form 1040, not 1040A or 1040EZ. You put your total win for the year (from all types of gambling, including live and online, added together) on the line "Other Income" and label it "Gross Gambling Income."

Married couples filing jointly combine their winning-session to-tals for the figure to put on the "Other Income" line. This again means adding all types of gambling together, even if the husband and wife play entirely different games.

But here comes the tricky part. You can claim a loss figure (for all types of gambling, live and online, added together) *only* if you itemize on Schedule A. Again, married couples that file jointly add their indi-vidual loss figures together for one total loss figure. You put the total allowed loss figure on Schedule A on a line in the section for "Other Miscellaneous Deductions" and label it "Gambling Losses to Extent of Gambling Income."

Did you notice I said total *allowed* loss figure? There's a restriction on listing your losses on Schedule A: You cannot reduce your tax on non-gambling income if you have more gambling losses than wins. The tax instructions put it quite clearly: *If you itemize your deductions on Schedule A, you can deduct gambling losses you had during the year, BUT ONLY UP TO THE AMOUNT OF YOUR WINNINGS* (emphasis added).

**MARISSA:** Here's an example. If your year-end winning total is $10,000 and your total loss is $20,000 (a net loss of $10,000), you may claim only a $10,000 deduction on Schedule A under "Other Deduc-tions." You cannot use the excess $10,000 to reduce non-gambling income.

Also, there's no carry-over to another year. This condition is stipu-lated in IRC section 165(d): *Losses from wagering transactions shall be allowed only to the extent of the gains from such transactions.* The courts have ruled time and time again that 165(d) does take precedence when applying tax law.

**JEAN:** The recreational gambler can feel real pain in the pocket-book because of IRS tax rules and procedures. Having to put your loss figure on Schedule A as a deduction isn't a problem for taxpayers who itemize anyway. However, a taxpayer forced to itemize only because of a large loss figure (to offset the large win figure in "Other Income") is losing the dollar amount of what would have been his standard deduction. Many find they need to figure it both ways, itemizing versus taking the standard deduction, to see which has the overall lowest tax obligation. (See the comparison of these two alternatives in the sample tax forms in Appendix B1 and B2.) If you do itemize, the one bright spot is that your loss figure isn't further limited as some other itemized deductions are.

However, there can be a far more severe punishment awaiting the recreational player because of the rule against netting out wins at the end of the year (subtracting gross losses from gross wins to report a net win only). Having to use a *gross* win figure on page 1 of your federal income tax form can put you in a higher AGI (adjusted gross income) category, where you'll be ineligible for certain benefits, such as IRA eligibility or education credits, and for some deductions that phase out as your AGI goes up. Seniors may find that they have to pay taxes on more of their Social Security income. You may even lose your exemption deductions. And to pour salt in the wound, many may live in an area where state and/or local taxes will be based on this higher AGI figure, a problem we discuss in Chapter 8.

Here's a comprehensive list of what can be affected negatively by having to include your *gross* gambling win figure in your adjusted gross income (AGI):

Social Security
Medicare premiums
IRA contributions
Mortgage interest deductions
Real estate taxes
Charitable contributions
Employee business expenses
Medical expense deductions
Rental real-estate deductions
Casualty loss deductions
Child tax credit
Earned income credit

DMV taxes (when the tax is based upon the value of the car)
Points on a home loan
Investment interest
Miscellaneous itemized deductions subject to the 2% limit
Lifetime learning credit
Hope credit
Retirement savings contribution credit
Adoption credit
Alternative Minimum Tax (AMT)

## THE PROFESSIONAL GAMBLER

**JEAN:** For some, the answer to the problems we just discussed is filing as a professional gambler, using Schedule C, Profit or Loss from Business (Sole Proprietorship). In this case, the gross-win figure for the year is put in Part I, Income. The gross loss figure for the year is put, with other business expenses, under Part II, Expenses, and subtracted from the gross win. This allows the much smaller net win to be carried over to page 1 of Form 1040, resulting in a lower AGI and avoiding some of the penalties we mentioned earlier. (See example in Appendix B3.)

However, filing as a professional gambler using Schedule C has its own set of problems. First, the IRS imposes rigid requirements on anyone wanting to claim gambling as his "business," although these are not all set in stone; individual situations are considered. However, court cases have established that your intent must be to make money as a primary source of income; it must not be just a hobby. The Supreme Court has defined a professional gambler as one who gambles "with regularity, continuity, and with an expectation of profit."

**MARISSA:** The landmark Supreme Court case that allowed gamblers to file as professionals was the case of Commissioner v. Groetzinger (see Appendix D). In that case, the Court concluded, "If one's gambling activity is pursued full time, in good faith, and with regularity, to the production of income for a livelihood, and is not a mere hobby, it is a trade or business within the meaning of the statutes with which we are here concerned." Essentially, the court ruled that each taxpayer's situation must be evaluated according to the *facts and circumstances* of the case.

Some people might think that if you make money at least three out of five years, you can automatically file as a business. However, many people make money in an avocation as well as in their vocation. You're probably still a recreational gambler unless you can meet the higher standard of being a professional. Being a professional is not just about winning; it's about showing that this activity is a major source of your income.

> *Nuclear physics is much easier than tax law. It's rational and always works the same way.*
>
> —Jerold Rochwald

## SHOWING A PROFIT

**MARISSA:** Some people misunderstand the "three-of-five" rule for Schedule C, making a profit three years out of five. One tax expert explained it this way: "A gambler who makes a profit in three (or more) of five tax years is entitled to a presumption, which the IRS can overcome, that he is in business; a gambler who doesn't has to overcome the contrary presumption."

One video poker player who understands the strict requirements to be a professional gambler put it this way: "Especially if your records show a loss, you'd better have a documented plan of what you're doing to correct the problem: switching to better games, changing to casinos with more cashback, playing more on double-point days, spending more time practicing on your computer, consulting with experts in your field, creating a better business plan. Don't laugh; courts and the IRS expect this! You'll be held to the same standard as any other self-employed person, plus you'll have to overcome the standard of 'personal pleasure that is derived from the activity.' (It's OK to enjoy what you do for a living, but a hobby is not a business.) Lack of records and a sound business plan are the biggest reasons for the denial of deductions.

"For example, one taxpayer deducted his expenses for his gold-mining trips to the Mojave Desert for 10 years. He'd kept perfect records, had a business plan, and consulted experts. Some years he made a buck, but mostly he didn't. A tax court ruled that since he was sincere in his attempt to make a go of it, his deductions were allowed. The court stated that 'a person can believe he can strike oil in Times Square, and while that may be far-fetched if not impossible, if he gets the best people and the best equipment and has a plan to accomplish his goal, this court will not and cannot judge how reasonable is his goal, only on his sincerity to accomplish it.'"

**JEAN:** You must spend "substantial" time conducting your gambling business; however, how many hours are "enough" would be evaluated on a case-by-case basis. Gambling income does not have to be your sole source of support, but a couple of trips a year to Las Vegas most likely won't be convincing.

Being business-like in your record-keeping is a must. For example, having a separate bank account for your playing bankroll and expenses will strengthen your case for being a pro.

**MARISSA:** Filing as a business is not necessarily an automatic good choice, even for a "big" gambler. It requires paying self-employment (SE) tax, in addition to your regular income taxes, if your net win is over $400. (A recreational gambler doesn't have to pay this SE tax, because his gambling win isn't categorized as "earned" income.) Self-employment tax is a hefty amount (about 15%) that can minimize or even wipe out the advantage you gain from filing Schedule C. (When you work for someone else, your employer picks up 50% of your Social Security contribution. When you're self-employed, you must pay it all.)

Another caveat here: You will not be entitled to all of the Schedule C advantages of taxpayers involved in businesses other than gambling. Schedule C filers normally may carry forward their losses. They can also offset losses against other income. Because IRC 165(d), which we quoted on page 44, takes precedence in determining gambling losses, the professional gambler is at a disadvantage when compared to other businesses. If you sell Amway and fail, you can use the net loss to offset other income. This is not permitted for any gambler, including professionals. As it has in many previous cases, the court ruled again, in Praytor v. Commissioner (2000), that claimed losses, even as a professional, may not exceed gains. That pesky Section 165(d) of the tax code takes precedence.

However, a 2008 IRS memo, which can be found at www.irs.gov/pub/irs-utl/am2008013.pdf, addresses the issue of whether *expenses* (as an issue separate from actual gambling losses) incurred by a professional gambler to engage in the business of gambling are subject to the limitation on deducting "losses from wagering transactions" in § 165(d) of the Internal Revenue Code.

The memorandum points out that there have been two divergent tracks of court cases pertaining to whether a professional gambler can deduct *expenses* in excess of gambling wins. I think eventually we'll see a court case, maybe even at the Supreme Court level, which will try to resolve the differences between these two highly differing opinions. For right now, deducting expenses in excess of your wins is a use-at-your-own-peril concept, since this memo is merely the opinion of one researcher at the IRS and plainly states: *This advice may not be used or cited as precedent.*

**JEAN:** There's a common belief among many tax professionals that filing as a professional gambler will increase the possibility of an audit, although no firm statistics support it. It *is* known that owning your own business and dealing in large amounts of cash are two things that can increase your chances of being audited. And the IRS' new emphasis on compliance and its plan to set up a new unit to deal exclusively with small businesses and the self-employed should certainly inspire professional gamblers to make sure they have very good records.

It's easier to meet the standards we have been talking about if one is a full-time professional gambler with no other jobs or other sources of income. But how about the retiree who is collecting Social Security or a pension and plays live poker full-time? Or how about the person who plays video poker 40 hours a week and works another full-time job, too? These issues are not as clear.

**MARISSA:** There have been court cases where the taxpayer who works a full-time job and also gambles full time has been allowed to file as a professional gambler. Barrish v. Commissioner (1984) is one example.

Another interesting and more recent case is Castagnetta v. Commissioner (2006). Castagnetta was a part-time truck driver and claimed on his taxes to be a professional gambler. He kept detailed records and also did extensive research in his area of gambling (horse racing). The court used a variety of factors to determine if he was in the "business of gambling." What won it for him was his methodical and business-like approach to the activity and the fact that he put in more than 40 hours a week on it. The drawback in this case is that this is only what's called a "summary opinion," so one cannot cite this case as precedent for other cases.

Thus, it may be possible for you to file as a professional gambler even if you don't meet every standard. However, you'll have to show that the profession of gambling is your primary one on as many levels as possible: time, earnings, expertise, etc.

**JEAN:** On the flip side, despite the stringent requirements and some disadvantages, there are many advantages to filing as a self-employed professional gambler, advantages that are afforded to anyone who has a business.

1. *Deduction of work-related expenses.* This might include such items as travel, tips, office supplies and equipment, professional fees, study books, classes/seminars, mileage, and Internet and cell phone us-

age. IRS Publication 535, *Business Expenses,* is a good resource to learn what deductions are allowed and their limitations. (An important note here: Your losses *plus* your expenses may not exceed your winnings; see discussion on page 49.)

2. *Earned income credit eligibility.* You might qualify for additional money given to low wage earners in those years you have minimal net gaming winnings.

3. *Self-employed health-insurance deductions.* As a self-employed individual, you may deduct your own health-insurance premiums. If you're married and hire your spouse as an employee, you can deduct your spouse's premium and the premium for the whole family, if applicable.

4. *Eligibility for Social Security and Medicare benefits.* Self-employment taxes are an expense now, but could be considered a future plus for many as a way to finance part of their retirement.

5. *Eligibility to set up a retirement plan to shelter income.* You can choose a SEP or an IRA or a solo 401(k). In the latter, for 2007 you can shelter up to $45,000 a year ($49,000 if you're over 50) and get a tax deduction that lowers AGI as well. (This figure is adjusted annually for inflation.)

**MARISSA:** One bright spot regarding filing as a professional gambler is that the IRS, in November 2002, issued a regulation stating that husband/wife partners in a business may be considered a "disregarded entity" in community-property states, such as California and Nevada. I believe this effectively allows husband/wife pros to offset their gambling wins/losses against each other. Therefore, spouses are no longer penalized if one is really lucky and the other one isn't. The other community-property states are Arizona, Idaho, Louisiana, New Mexico, Texas, West Virginia, and Wisconsin.

**JEAN:** A warning. You may not always have a choice in how you file; you might be required to file as self-employed, utilizing forms 1040, Schedule C, and Schedule SE, if the IRS feels you fit into the category of professional gambler. This has caught up with a few gamblers who collected a large number of W-2Gs or who tried to switch back to filing as a recreational gambler after having filed as a business for one or more years.

**MARISSA:** And I have another warning. The IRS has a propensity to want to have it both ways. They've displayed this attitude when it comes to the issue of employee compensation within close corporations and they display this attitude when it comes to gamblers. If you have large losses and file as a professional, the IRS will try to classify you as a recreational gambler. Conversely, if you report a large net win, they'll try to classify you as a professional gambler. That's why it's important to seek the advice and assistance of a tax professional, should you ever be contacted by the IRS about your filing status.

*"The taxpayer—that's someone who works for the federal government, but doesn't have to take a civil-service examination."*

—Ronald Reagan

# 5
# Federal Government Issues

**JEAN:** It's no surprise to anyone, I imagine, that the federal government is interested in what happens in a casino—or anywhere else where gambling occurs. And there's probably no governmental department that's more interested in your money than the IRS. And where there's government, there's paperwork.

## THE W-2G

Gamblers, if they know anything about gambling paperwork, are probably most familiar with the IRS form W-2G (the G stands for gambling) that applies to "Certain Gambling Winnings." This is the tax form that any for-profit organization issues you—and sends a copy to the IRS—when you win a specified amount while gambling. (Churches and other non-profit organizations are exempt from issuing W-2Gs.) Go to Appendix A1 to examine a sample form.

Most people don't know that there are different rules for when a W-2G must be issued, depending on the form of gambling. For horse and dog racing, jai alai, state lotteries, and some other kinds of wagering, this form must be given for any winnings that are at least 300 times the amount of the bet. However, there's a special rule for bingo and slot machines: You get a W-2G for a *gross* win that's $1,200 or more, no matter how much your original bet was. And to make it more complicated, keno has its own special rule: a W-2G for any *net* win of $1,500 or more.

A player will receive a W-2G for a *single* winning table-game bet if *both* of the following apply:
1. The payout is $600 or more *and*
2. The winnings are paid at 300-to-1 (or higher).

Some examples would be progressives on Caribbean Stud and Fortune Pai Gow and some bonus bets on Let It Ride.

An important note on W-2G rules for machine play: You don't get a W-2G when you cash out more than $1,200 on a slot machine after a period of play. It's required only for the win of $1,200 or more on *one* hand or spin. I've heard of players who've had to explain this to green casino employees, especially in Indian casinos.

Also, on multi-line machines, all line winners on one "play" are totaled together and are usually considered one *hand*. For example, on the usual non-progressive quarter Triple Play machine, a dealt royal gives you a $1,000 win on each of the three lines. When multi-line first came out, there was confusion on this issue. Sometimes it was treated as three separate hands and no W-2G was issued. Occasionally, you might find a casino that still does it this way. However, the common practice is to consider all lines together as one hand, and in this example, you'd be issued a W-2G for $3,000.

**MARISSA:** The reporting figures mentioned above were established in the '70s and have not been updated to account for inflation and the introduction of high-denomination and multi-line machines. However, if you stick with quarter machines, you may have to stop for this sometimes maddeningly slow W-2G paperwork only once in a while, i.e., the infrequent top jackpot on slots or on a progressive video poker machine. But if you play at the $1-or-higher levels, you can be held up quite often when the machine locks up, you dig for ID, and you have to wait until the W-2G shows up.

Fortunately, casinos are allowed to keep a log of a player's W-2G payoffs for higher-denomination machines and can issue one form covering the total at the end of play in one session or on one day. This is sometimes called being put "on session" or "on the board" (because the log is kept on a clipboard). And if you're playing in the lofty high-limit salons, such as on a 5-coin $100 Jacks or Better video poker machine, you trigger a W-2G anytime you hit 3-of-a-kind or above. In that case, you're assigned one employee who sits beside you as long as you're playing and records each $1,200 payoff you hit.

Don't look for the feds to raise the $1,200 threshold that triggers a W-2G for a machine jackpot. With the non-compliance of gamblers is already widespread, plus the fact that "sin activities" always provide good taxation targets, we're much more likely to see them require more restricting paperwork.

**JEAN:** Both players and casinos harbor some widespread misconceptions about W-2Gs. First, most players believe (or want to believe) that if you don't get a W-2G, you don't have to report that particular gambling win. And this viewpoint is supported by information in print, even from otherwise accurate gambling writers, seeming to encourage players to look for a machine with a top jackpot under $1,200.

Surprisingly, even the casinos seem to encourage this kind of thinking. I've seen many slot machines with a $1,199 top jackpot that seems to give the appearance of circumventing tax law. Some casinos have reduced the payoffs slightly on some winning video poker hands, so the jackpot is just under the W-2G-issuing amount of $1,200, such as a $5 machine that drops the regular payoff of 250 credits ($1,250) for the straight flush to 239 ($1,195). Or they create a high-limit slot machine that replaces W-2G-generating jackpots on a primary game with lots of bonus wins on a secondary one, keeping each one under that paperwork $1,200 figure.

One casino went so far as to rename some of its VP machines where management had fiddled with the schedules so there were fewer W-2G jackpots. They even sent out press releases, touting the new "duty-free" machines: Duty-Free Double Bonus and Duty-Free Double Double Bonus. I'm not sure whether the short tenure of these games was due to a lack of play or the casino's realization that it might not be wise to promote so obviously the erroneous idea that they could eliminate your tax liability. It's one thing to try to cut out cumbersome paperwork and irritatingly long delays for your customer; it's another to encourage them to break the law.

No matter how shrewdly gambling writers and casinos may seem to be steering you down a different and dangerous path, you're responsible for reporting all gambling wins, and whether you get a W-2G or not has no bearing on that. The fact that many people don't report gambling wins when there's no W-2G evidence won't help you in an IRS audit.

---

**JEAN:** There have always been "ten-percenters" hanging around dog and horse tracks and casino race/sports books—guys who had little income of their own and, therefore, ordinarily didn't pay income taxes. They'd cash for someone a winning ticket that was high enough to generate a W-2G, assuming the tax liability of the win (which usually would be little or none for them) for a 10% commission or "tip."

Sometimes you'll see "volunteers" sitting around poker rooms, especially near the end of a tournament, willing to claim your winnings for you. They give you their name and Social Security number for your W-2G, because they say that they have plenty of losses. What's the catch? They want a percentage of your winnings in cash.

**MARISSA:** Of course, we need to point out, although it's probably obvious, that none of this is legal. Technically, it's tax evasion and perjury.

**JEAN:** What if you don't keep a gambling diary and you have one or more W-2Gs from slot machine jackpots that were $1,200 or more? Can you just count these as your gross win? Probably thousands, even hundreds of thousands, of people do this every year and don't get audited by the IRS. Why not? In the majority of these cases, people are actually paying more in taxes than they would have if they'd kept the required records and kept track, as we talked about in Chapter 2, of all their gambling session wins and losses separately. A W-2G jackpot total is not the same as a winning-session total; all truthful gamblers readily admit that they don't always end up a session with the whole jackpot intact. In fact, many are the days when Brad and I get a W-2G or two and end up with our total for the day's session in the loss column.

**MARISSA:** The other problem with using your W-2G totals as your win totals, without any yearly diary, is that if you're audited, the IRS may question you about other gambling sessions. They'll assume you had other winning sessions when no W-2G was issued and will start looking for other evidence. You say you lost on all the other days? The burden of proof for losses is squarely in your lap, and although you may be able to get some kind of statements from casinos, these may not always be accepted as proof without a detailed diary. Tax-court decisions have supported the idea that gambling records are much more believable when they include both W-2G and non-W-2G wins.

**JEAN:** An important warning here. You don't have to include W-2G forms with your return unless tax has been withheld. However, if you don't use your W-2G total as your actual gross-win total (or if your gross-win total is less than the W-2G total), you must be sure to make a list of all your W-2Gs and gambling-related 1099s and attach it to your income-tax return, with the explanation that these amounts have been included in your session win/loss records. Otherwise, you're likely to get caught in the government's computer-run "Information Reporting Program." A computer, when it's matching up various reporting forms (i.e., W-2Gs and 1099s) to returns with the same Social

Security number, will kick out your return if it can't find that you accounted for these amounts, and you'll get a letter informing you that you owe taxes on the difference.

This isn't a full-fledged IRS audit, but what's called a "letter audit." Still, it's always scary to find a letter from the IRS in your mailbox, especially one that states you owe more money, sometimes a lot more. One year I forgot this list of W-2Gs with my return and got such a notice, but a simple letter of explanation with the list of W-2Gs solved the problem quickly. I wasn't even asked to produce my diary.

**MARISSA:** These letters that Jean is referring to are called CP-2000 letters. They're sent when the information reported on a tax return does not match other information that the IRS has collected, e.g., the W-2Gs. Unfortunately, when you respond with an explanation, the IRS employees who review them are usually entry-level personnel who know little or nothing about the taxation of gambling. Add the fact that they're overworked and too often this becomes a frustrating paperwork battle. If letters of explanation and phone calls don't solve the problem, you may be forced to hire a professional to fight the battle for you. Or if the disputed amount is not too large, you may simply pay it to make the problem go away. We discuss this problem further in Chapter 7, which you should read if you have any questions about whether you should use your winning-sessions total on the "Other Income" line 21 on page 1 of your return or your W2-G total.

**JEAN:** Be diligent in hanging on to all your W-2Gs, or at least keep a list of every one you're given. This is a warning from a high-roller's painful experience: "If you lose or misplace any of the hundreds of W-2Gs the casino issues you for qualifying jackpots and don't account for them on your tax return, the government will charge you interest and you'll have to submit an amended tax return that will take months to settle."

**MARISSA:** I'd like to add to that. Don't rely solely on W-2Gs to have an idea as to how much tax you should pay. IRS rules state that

# W-2Gs on Cruise Ships

**JEAN:** Many years ago you'd never get W-2Gs from casinos onboard ships, but now most cruise ships issue them to American citizens and permanent American residents on wins of more than $1,199 on machines, the same as land-based casinos do. Apparently, this is a policy change since 9/11 and is a result of the Patriot Act. Of course, as we've emphasized in other chapters, all gambling wins are required to be reported, whether or not any paperwork is issued.

Although each cruise line has its own policies on this subject, the following information from the Norwegian Cruise Line "Casinos at Sea" Web page, www.nclcasino.com/faq.htm, gives some helpful information:

"The Federal Income Tax Act stipulates that all American citizens and Permanent Residents are subject to global income tax. Regardless if a U.S. citizen or Permanent Resident earns this income in international waters or with a ship that carries a foreign flag, if income is generated, such income becomes taxable. If a Social Security number is furnished, then the document W-2G will be issued with *no* upfront tax deduction. If a Social Security number is not furnished, then an upfront withholding tax will apply. Foreign guests will be taxed only if winnings are derived within U.S. domestic waters. Whenever a tax form is issued to the guest, a duplicate copy will be sent to the IRS. "

extensions extend the time to *file* only, not the time to *pay*. Therefore, if your records aren't in order by the tax deadline, you should still send in enough money to cover your tax liability. Any shortfall will be charged a "failure-to-pay" penalty and interest. However, with a properly filed extension, there's no "failure-to-timely-file" penalty, which is much higher.

If you've lost some W-2Gs and 1099s and haven't kept a list, you can request by phone that the IRS mail or fax you a complete record of them. There's no charge for this service, but it may take some time for them to respond. They don't send you duplicate copies, but just a list, with the name of the payer, date issued, and amount. If you need them quickly, some filers have been successful in obtaining records from their local IRS offices, but I suggest you don't try this on April 14th! More often than not, the IRS won't have complete information in their computers until around August, so if you need this information to file your return, you'd better send in the form asking for an extension *and* include a generous best estimate of the tax that will be due to avoid any penalties and interest charges.

*"Taxes: Of life's two certainties, the only one for which you can get an automatic extension."*

—Anonymous

## INCOME TAX WITHHOLDING

**JEAN:** Federal tax withholding is not required for any amount of winnings from slot machines, bingo, and keno for U.S. citizens who have proper ID and give a Social Security number. However, you may request withholding by the casino for any amount, a handy technique at times to save you the extra paperwork of filing estimated taxes. Casinos will usually do this for you with no problems, but occasionally I've had this request refused, because the particular employee wasn't

The slot machine manufacturer IGT has brought out a new video poker machine called "Guaranteed Play." It has this note on it: "Non-U.S. citizens or players without valid ID must pay U.S. withholding tax which may require an early cashout and the loss of any remaining poker hands in the event of a jackpot of $1,200 or more."

familiar with the procedure or didn't want to bother with it.

Federal withholding tax (25%-31%) is required for most other forms of gambling, usually payouts of more than $5,000 that are at least 300 times the amount wagered. However, the IRS gave a new withholding wrinkle to the poker world just before this book went to press in September 2007. They issued Revenue Procedure 2007-57, which states that starting March 8, 2008, there will be a mandatory 25% withholding on all U.S. poker-tournament wins when the money received exceeds the entry and buy-in fees by $5,000. Fortunately soon after, negotiations between the casino industry and the IRS resulted in the IRS rescinding this requirement in favor of new stricter rules for issuing W-2Gs. Go to Chapter 6 for more details.

A reminder: Don't forget to account for any tax withheld from W-2G jackpots on your tax return.

**MARISSA:** A common misconception is that if you hit a big jackpot, so big that you have no reasonable chance of losing it all back that year, you have to send the government an estimated tax payment or be hit with a penalty. That's not always the case. Perhaps the withholding from your other income is enough to satisfy the IRS requirement for most people: that you send in each year either 90% of the current year's liability or 100% of the previous year's liability in order to avoid being assessed a withholding penalty.

## A Withholding Tip from an Internet Friend

"Requesting withholding can do more than just save time on paperwork. If you've underwithheld or underpaid estimated taxes during the year, having taxes withheld from a jackpot can save you money in penalties and interest. Withholding at any point during the year is treated as if it's been done equally throughout the year. Theoretically, therefore, if you've underpaid your estimated taxes by $5,000 during the year, on December 31 you could go to a $5 machine and have every W-2G payment withheld until you made up the $5,000, thereby eliminating any underwithholding penalties you might have incurred."

(**JEAN:** Of course, this might be a more expensive option in the long run, unless you get lucky fast and win.)

## SOCIAL SECURITY NUMBERS

"A couple of years ago, a friend hit a $2,000 royal flush at an Indian casino in Wisconsin. He did not carry his Social Security card with him and, as a result, they wouldn't pay him anything. They did allow him to return later with the card and get his money, but it proved to be a huge hassle."

"One casino in Florida will withhold federal income tax if you cannot present a valid Social Security card—no exceptions—they wouldn't even take my valid military ID card with SSN and photo on it."

"A few years ago my wife hit a jackpot for $2,500 at an Indian casino in New Mexico. She did not have her government-issued Social Security card. She did have her driver's license and her passport with the Social Security number on it. They wouldn't take any Social Security info without the official card. After about an hour's wait, they gave her a W-2G, but only paid her 60% of the win value, the rest being withheld for federal income taxes."

**JEAN:** The horror stories pour in when the subject of Social Security numbers and casinos is brought up on Internet gambling forums. We all know that identity theft is a big problem and we've been warned not to carry anything that has our Social Security number on it. But the message hasn't seemed to get to some casinos.

The fact is that there's no federal or state law that requires a U.S. citizen to give *printed proof* of his Social Security number in order to be issued a W-2G and paid a jackpot. He can provide it verbally or write it down. But you may ask how the casino can be sure that a customer gives the correct number. The IRS has provided a form they can give to the player, a W-9 form, *Request for Taxpayer Identification Number and Certification.* By signing this form, you are certifying, under penalties of perjury, that this is your Social Security number.

I hear your next question already. No, you don't have to give your Social Security number, but in that case, the IRS requires that the casino withhold 28% of the winnings for federal income tax.

As shown by the stories at the beginning of this section, some casinos seem to mix up Social Security cards and ID cards. You *do* have to show a valid ID or the casino can refuse to pay off a W-2G jackpot until you do. You do *not* have to show your original Social Security card. In fact, it is written right on your Social Security card that it is not be used as identification.

What can you do if a casino doesn't seem to be following the IRS rules and requires an original Social Security card? I'd ask to speak to a supervisor or even a senior casino executive. One player suggested carrying W-9 forms with you (they can be printed out from the IRS website) and giving one to the casino employee making this mistaken request. He said that some new and/or small casinos, especially Native American ones, do not seem to know about this option.

## BIG BROTHER IS WATCHING YOU

**JEAN:** There's more government paperwork required from casinos than just the W-2Gs and 1099s we discussed earlier. Casinos are required to do other types of reporting to the government to fulfill new anti-money-laundering rules. Some players, for example, think (hope?) that if they stay under the now-famous $10,000 limit for cash transactions, they're safe. However, casinos have special requirements that trigger reports at lower amounts.

Note that there's also been a change in Nevada. Regulation 6A, a Nevada statute that had slightly different rules for Nevada casinos, expired on July 1, 2007. Nevada casinos are now classified as financial institutions—just like banks—and follow the Title 31 rules for MSBs (Money Service Businesses) at the federal level, which casinos in other states have been following for years.

**MARISSA:** In this post-9/11 era, we must all be aware of the USA Patriot Act. The $10,000 that Jean just referred to is not just a one-time transaction requisite. A casino must keep track of one person's transactions that total $10,000 in cash-in or cash-out in a 24-hour period and fill out a Currency Transaction Report (CTR).

This is a huge tracking problem for a large casino, where customers may be playing many different games, buying and cashing in chips all over the place, and/or taking markers and cashing out for multiple smaller amounts. Therefore, a casino is required to record many single transactions below $10,000. According to Title 31, when recording a transaction of $3,000 to $10,000, the casino employee must verify and record customer information, including ID; record transaction information, including the amount, date, and serial numbers if exchanging cash for travelers checks; and retain the record for five years from the date of the transaction.

Again, as mentioned earlier, the casino is not required to record your Social Security number on the CTR for amounts less than $10,000, but that won't stop them from asking. It's unlikely that a cash transaction of between $3,000 and $10,000 will be denied if you don't supply a SSN, but that assumes the casino employee is completely conversant with the new regulations.

In addition, any financial-institution employee, and that includes those in casinos, is required to fill out a SAR (Suspicious Activity Report) for any cash transaction over $2,000 if, in his opinion, it looks to be "suspicious." This form goes to the FINCEN (Financial Crimes Enforcement Network), the U.S. Treasury Department's financial-crimes tracking organization. You might suspect that this form is being filled out if you're asked for your ID and Social Security number. However, casinos aren't required to inform you that they're filing a government report if they already have this information about you (e.g., from a players card application or previous W-2Gs), so you won't necessarily know when you're being watched and reported on. In fact, in some cases, the casinos are *forbidden* to inform you that they're reporting some of your personal gambling information to a government agency.

## GAMBLING ISSUES FOR NON-U.S. CITIZENS

**JEAN:** The rules for taxation and withholding tax for non-resident-alien (NRA) gamblers vary, depending on the tax treaties in force between their countries and the U.S. As I write this in the summer of 2007, the IRS lists the following countries whose residents are exempt from U.S taxation on gambling income: Austria, Czech Republic, Denmark, Finland, France, Germany, Hungary, Ireland, Italy, Japan, Latvia, Lithuania, Luxembourg, Netherlands, Russian Federation, Slovak Republic, Slovenia, South Africa, Spain, Sweden, Tunisia, Turkey, Ukraine, and the United Kingdom. (In addition, there is no U.S. tax for any non-resident from any foreign country on wins from blackjack, baccarat, craps, roulette, or the big-6 wheel in the United States.)

All non-residents will be issued paperwork, not a W-2G, but a

Form 1042-S, *Foreign Person's U.S. Source Income Subject to Withholding*. It depends on the terms of their countries' treaties with the U.S., but most of these non-residents must have U.S. income tax withheld, usually at a rate of 30% of the gross amount of the win. Non-residents from countries with a no-taxation treaty should not depend on the casino to have up-to-date treaty information, and there is a form they should always carry to show the casino in case of a big win, Form W-8BEN, *Certificate of Foreign Status of Beneficial Owner for United States Tax Withholding*. Although they will still get paperwork, no tax will be withheld.

I saw an example first-hand when Bob McKeown, "Dateline's" on-camera correspondent and a Canadian citizen, hit a W-2G-size jackpot as I was teaching him on camera the correct way to play video poker while NBC was filming a story about Brad's and my life in Las Vegas. If I had been playing the machine, I would have received a W-2G and no tax would have been withheld. Bob received a 1042-S and was paid only 70% of what I would have been paid.

This story brings up to a common question for foreign visitors to our casinos: Is there any way to get back the U.S. tax withheld?

Some non-residents, again depending on which country they come from, have the option of getting back some or all of the amount withheld, but to do so they have to file a non-resident tax form with the IRS, Form 1040NR. However, as I described in earlier chapters and just as for U.S citizens, they must have good records in order to itemize their losses to offset their winnings. Therefore, I suggest that non-residents, especially those who often gamble in the U.S., keep a gaming log. You never know when you'll get lucky and win a jackpot big enough for Uncle Sam to take a piece.

Another smart thing a non-resident should do before beginning to gamble in the U.S. is to apply for an Individual Taxpayer Identification Number (ITIN). This number is the equivalent of a resident's Social Security number and can be given to a casino when hitting a jackpot that requires the 1042-S form that I described above. You could wait to see if you do hit a jackpot, but then your 1042-S would not have this number on it. You're required to have an ITIN if you want to file a 1040NR form for a refund of the withholding tax, and it's much simpler if the IRS can match up all documents with the same ITIN number.

The easiest way to get an ITIN is to apply for it while you're in the U.S. You can download Form W-7, *Application for IRS Individual Taxpayer Identification Number,* from the IRS website and take the completed form and your ID requirements (such as a passport) to an IRS office. There's no charge for this. Or you can apply at a U.S. embassy. You can also apply by mail as long as you submit certified copies of documents, such as a passport. You can get your documents certified at a U.S. consulate, but there may be a charge for this.

There are also "jackpot-recovery" companies that will help you with filing forms and obtaining the ITIN. Fees for this service tend to be high, usually 25%-30%, but sometimes as high as 50% of amounts recovered. However, this may be worth it to some people, because part of their service includes dealing with casino accounting departments and obtaining win/loss data.

Some years ago, Canada and the U.S changed their tax treaty so that Canadians could get a refund of U.S taxes withheld from jackpots. Here's an excerpt from the IRS website, which uses Canada as an illustration of how many non-residents can get a refund of withholding tax. It's a fairly simple straightforward procedure.

Q: "I won money at a Las Vegas casino and my winnings were subject to a 30% withholding tax. I am a Canadian citizen. How can I get the withholding tax back?"

A: "Generally, you must file a tax return to claim a refund of withholding. Gambling winnings by nonresidents of the U.S. are taxed at a flat 30% tax rate. However, under the U.S./Canada Tax Treaty, residents of Canada may claim gambling losses, but only to the extent of gambling winnings. You should report both your total gambling winnings and your total gambling losses on page 4 of Form 1040NR, *U.S. Nonresident Alien Income Tax Return,* on the dotted portion of line 79. If you have net gambling winnings (after offsetting your total losses against your total winnings), you should include this net amount on line 79, column (d) of the Form 1040NR. You should also attach a copy of the Form 1042-S, *Foreign Person's U.S. Source Income Subject to Withholding,* showing the taxes withheld, to your Form 1040NR."

Items to check on the IRS website for more information:

1. Publication 515, *Withholding of Tax on Nonresident Aliens and Foreign Corporations*

2. Publication 519, *U.S. Tax Guide for Aliens*

3. Publication 901, *U.S. Tax Treaties*

4. Publication 1915, *Understanding Your IRS Individual Taxpayer Identification Number*

5. Form W-7 IRS, *Application for Individual Taxpayer Identification Number*

6. Form 1040NR, *U.S. Nonresident Income Tax Return*

*"People who complain about taxes can be divided into two classes: men and women."*

—Anonymous

# 6
# Tax Help for the Poker Player

**JEAN:** Although poker players inhabit two different venues, on-line and live games, I need to emphasize that the tax implications are much the same for players in both. Also, most of what Marissa and I've said in the first five chapters to gamblers in general also applies to poker players.

Let's review the basics we covered earlier, and then we'll consider each one as it impacts the poker player.

1. The IRS states that all gambling wins must be declared as income *from whatever source derived.* This includes home games, gambling in cyberspace, when you get no paperwork from the source, or even if you're gambling in an illegal venue. Read Chapter 1 for discussion of these issues.

2. The IRS specifically states that gamblers must keep a record of winnings and losses, and you may not net out one win/loss figure for the whole year. Recreational players must report winning sessions as income on their tax returns, and if they want to list losses, these are reported separately as deductions. Gambling record-keeping is discussed

in detail in Chapter 2. These IRS rules can cause major problems for residents of some states with onerous state-return requirements. We talk about those problems in Chapter 8.

3. The subject of tournaments, drawings, and comps brings up new questions for the gambler. Which ones are considered income? What forms will the casino issue you? How do you handle Form 1099 wins on your tax return? We discuss all those subjects in Chapter 3, as well as how to handle gambling wins when you partner up with another person or belong to a group.

4. You may file a tax return as a recreational or a professional player, but the IRS has imposed rigid requirements for the latter. We discuss the problems in making this decision, with the pros and cons of each, in Chapter 4.

5. The government can get involved in your gambling activity, whether you want it to or not. In Chapter 5 we discuss casino paperwork, protecting your Social Security number, tax withholding rules, tax issues for non-U.S. citizens, and what financial information the government requires casinos to collect.

## POKER REPORTING AND RECORD-KEEPING

**MARISSA:** Let's look at Jean's first item above, about gambling winnings as income. In U.S. casinos, W-2Gs are required to be filed with the government when certain payouts are reached, the amount depending on the IRS rules for a particular kind of game. However, poker isn't mentioned. Therefore, poker players rarely get casino paperwork for most non-tournament play.

Likewise, online casinos and card rooms, since they're outside U.S. jurisdiction, don't issue W-2Gs for any win.

But just because you don't get a W-2G or the information is not reported to the IRS doesn't mean that you don't have to report it. Not reporting it constitutes tax evasion.

Some gamblers question whether they can delay counting on-line winnings until they actually withdraw the money. I talked about the concept of constructive receipt when we were discussing casino cashback in Chapter 3. I gave the example of the bank that gives you interest on your savings; it counts as income even though you don't withdraw it from your account. The same principle holds true for on-line winnings; if there are no restrictions for you to withdraw it, that money is income.

Too many poker players have been thinking that there's no way the government can find out about their online gambling. Think again. *There's always a paper trail.* No matter how many foreign bank or on-line accounts you have, your U.S. bank accounts and financial trans-actions, plus your noticeable assets, may give the IRS strong leads to unreported gambling income. Also, many are finding that the retroac-tive action the government took in 2000, obtaining MasterCard and American Express card transactions billed to bank accounts in some offshore "tax-havens," is now being used against NETeller, a major money-transfer agent for online gambling.

**JEAN:** As I said in the first chapter, the fact that all gambling ac-tion is to be reported makes the question moot, at least in the taxation area, about whether online gambling is legal or not, no matter how long it takes for this to be decided by the U.S government, if it ever really does become clear-cut. Some people who earn income at illegal activities (i.e., prostitution, bookmaking, etc.) report that income on their tax returns to avoid prosecution for tax evasion. Remember, it was easier for the government to put away Al Capone for tax evasion rather than for the violent crimes he committed.

**MARISSA:** Jean's second point is about record-keeping and brings up the basic question about what constitutes a gambling "session." "Session" is never defined in any IRS document, so Jean and I strived for some sensible general answers in Chapter 2. How these apply to poker players depends on whether they play in cash games, often called "ring" games, or in tournaments.

Essentially, the casual non-tournament live or online poker player treats the time spent in one game at one table as a session. Yesterday, I sat down (at a live or virtual table) at 3 p.m. with $100 and left the game at 4 p.m. with $200. Hence, that's a $100 "winning session." Today, I sit down with $100 and walk away with nothing. Hence, that's a $100 "losing session." Pretty simple and straightforward, isn't it?

**JEAN:** But there can be more than one way to look at a session for someone who plays long hours and jumps from game to game or plays online in several games at one time. Is the net win/loss for each type of game, i.e., all your Texas hold 'em play, lumped together as one session and the same for all your Omaha play if you switch back and forth tables without cashing in your chips? Or do you divide your sessions by betting levels? Or do you count a session beginning from when you first buy chips and ending when you cash in your chips, even though you've moved from table to table and game to game?

Perhaps you feel like a shopkeeper who adds up the register totals at the end of each day and choose the "whole-day" session.

The marathon player may have a session that covers a couple of days of non-stop poker and no sleep.

In any case, a session ends when a player cashes in his chips and/or leaves a casino poker room (for anything other than a short break) or signs off from a virtual casino.

**MARISSA:** As we discussed at length in Chapter 2, in an audit, the session method you use, in the absence of specific IRS guidance, has to be based on consistency, reasonableness, and practicality and depends on the circumstances in each individual case. The more conservative you are, the finer you should define a session. The most conservative definition (and the safest in an audit) for a poker player is to treat each table at which you play as an individual session. Although that sounds like a record-keeping challenge, it really isn't. There are great computer programs on the market that can keep track of your wins and losses by table. (*Poker Tracker* is by far the best and most recognized program on the market.)

**JEAN:** If you choose to have a written log rather than a computer program, here are some of the things you might want to put in it.

date
name of casino and/or location
name of game or tournament ID
time in
time out
total time played
buy-ins
cash-outs
total win/loss

**MARISSA:** Fortunately, a "session" for a tournament player is usually more clear-cut than for a ring-game player, whether it's a sit-n-go tournament of one or two tables that starts when enough players register, or a multi-table tournament, which is usually held at various specified times throughout the day (or many days) for different buy-in amounts. Each separate tournament (no matter how long it runs) is a separate session. If you win money, then it's a winning session. If you get knocked out before the money, your entry fee is your loss. If you play a $10 satellite where you win an entry into a $100 tournament, I'd consider winning the entry a $90 win. Then, if you bust out of that $100 tournament, I'd consider that to be a $100 loss.

Bottom line, whether it's a tournament or a ring game, you'll need to spend perhaps 15 minutes every poker day on record-keeping. That's a necessity for all gamblers, but it's especially true for the poker player. You're much better off spending a few minutes taking care of your tax business now than paying me a lot of money to figure it out later!

## POKER PAPERWORK

**JEAN:** Much less paperwork is issued to a poker player who plays only in ring games than, for example, to the casino machine player. There are no W-2Gs or 1099s, even in high-stakes games, except occasionally in some (but not all) casinos for bad-beat payoffs or other side promotions.

No record is kept by the casino of what games you played, or at what table limits, or how many hours you played, except perhaps for the purpose of granting comps or qualifying for a promotion, such as a freeroll. The casino does keep track of chip buy-ins and cash-outs with dates, times, and amounts. However, a casino is unlikely to want to dig through its records to give you any verification of the details of your play. This information should be kept in your log.

Keep in mind that because of these chip buy-in and cash-out records, the cash-game poker player doesn't escape the attention of Big Brother. As we discussed in Chapter 5, in addition to the familiar Currency Transaction Report (CTR) reporting requirements of cash-in or cash-out transactions of more than $10,000 in one 24-hour period, the newer Patriot Act has special requirements for casinos that trigger government reports at $3,000. And any financial-institution employee is required to fill out a Suspicious Activity Report on a transaction of $2,000 or more if it looks fishy.

**MARISSA:** In Jean's third point at the beginning of the chapter, she mentions tournaments. Casino-paperwork rules for poker tournaments are often different from those for tournaments in other casino games, where the winners usually get a 1099 form for a payoff of more than $600. I say usually, because, as we discussed in Chapter 3, this is not standard with all casinos. And this non-conformity is even greater in the arena of poker tournaments.

In theory, tournaments are just ring games where all the players put their money into the pot and the last person remaining wins the pot. But that's not how the IRS views it. In most (but not all) cardrooms today, you receive a W-2G if you win more than $600 in a tournament. The peculiar thing is that satellite tournaments aren't considered "tournaments" by the IRS and, therefore, no W-2Gs are issued, even though satellite-tournament prizes can be as high as $10,000.

Of course, to beat the same drum we've been pounding throughout the book, if you win money playing in a poker tournament, you're required to report it as income. Having no paperwork may lead you to be tempted not to report it on your tax return. However, I'd definitely caution against that, since tournament winners are public information on a number of websites, such as Cardplayer.com and the Hendon Mob database at www.hendonmob.com.

Why are there so many different policies on the paperwork for poker tournaments? First, poker wasn't mentioned in IRS Revenue Procedure 77-29 (in Appendix C), which outlines the requirements for issuing a W-2G for many games. There's no law or regulation to insure uniformity for poker paperwork. So some casinos and cardrooms have asked the IRS for a private letter ruling, and others have had rules imposed on them when being investigated by the IRS. Others have merely consulted their private tax advisors and then made up their own policies.

**JEAN:** Casino tax withholding policies are fairly standard. Federal taxes aren't withheld from poker-tournament payoffs to U.S. citizens, no matter how large the win, unless the player requests it, as many do to save the trouble of filing and paying estimated tax. However, many professional poker players in the U.S. who come from other countries have 30% withheld from poker-tournament wins, depending on the tax treaties that their countries have with the U.S. In Chapter 5 we discuss at length the gambling issues for non-U.S. citizens and list the countries whose residents currently do not have to pay taxes on U.S. gambling income. We also give information on how to get back some or all of the tax withheld.

It isn't just federal tax requirements that poker players have to deal with. Some states require that the casino withhold state taxes from

W-2G gambling wins. I've heard that at least some casinos in Indiana follow the rules for machine jackpots when they pay out poker-tournament money, issuing W-2Gs and withholding the same 3.4% state tax for wins of $1,200 or more. Go to Chapter 8 to see how many states punish gamblers, including poker players, by requiring that they report gross wins as income, but allow no deduction for losses, even if the taxpayers can deduct them on their federal returns.

## POKER GAMBLING GROUPS

**MARISSA:** We cover gambling groups in Chapter 3 and, actually, you find this phenomenon more prevalent in poker than in any other game, especially over the last few years. Tournaments are springing up all over the world and the entry fees alone prevent all but the most heavily bankrolled to enter a number of them regularly. And even many of the well-heeled poker professionals like to dilute their risk. So sometimes the most skilled sell a "piece" of themselves or have a financial backer. Or several pros will form a group to share all their wins. Often, a few amateurs will pool their money to come up with an entry fee for a tournament in which one of their group will play and the whole group will split whatever winnings he earns.

Form 5754, *Statement by Person(s) Receiving Gambling Winnings,* is available for poker players to use for partnerships and group arrangements. (See the instructions and filled-out example of Form 5754 in Appendix A3.) This is an official form, filled out by the actual tournament winner and given to the casino, which allows it to issue W-2Gs to each member of the group for his or her part of a win, rather than giving the one winner a W-2G for the total amount.

However, poker players face the same problem that we talked about in Chapter 3 in terms of machine team play. Many casinos won't accept Form 5754, even though the instructions on the form say you "must" give it to them in some situations: *You must complete Form 5754 if you receive gambling winnings either for someone else or as a member of a group of winners on the same winning ticket. The information you provide on the form enables the payer of the winnings to prepare Form W-2G, Certain Gambling Winnings, for each winner to show the winnings taxable to each.*

No one likes to upset a casino, even when he feels he's in the right. So, as we did in Chapter 3, we give you an option: The one W-2G jackpot winner issues 1099s to each of the partners for the agreed-upon share.

**JEAN:** Another kind of group activity in poker, usually just in smaller tournaments, is called a "chop," which is simply an agreement among two or more remaining players to divide up the prize money and discontinue play. Most casinos will distribute the prize money per the instructions of the players who agree to the chop and issue individual tax paperwork for the amount each player actually received.

I heard of an unusual "renegotiation" of an announced prize structure. At a small Vegas locals casino that offered a regular tournament, the actual tournament was rarely played. Qualifying players, all of whom knew each other, simply cut up the total prize money equally. I'm assuming that they all wanted to go home and get to bed early!

Advice for poker players (as well as those in any other game) who want to form or participate in a gambling group: *Get all the terms in writing before any gambling is done.* You may have heard the old saw: "Oral contracts aren't worth the paper they aren't written on."

Actually, my husband and I recently broke this rule when we went into a big slot tournament (described in Chapter 3) with only an oral agreement, with our best friends, and then Brad scooped the half-million-dollar first prize. Everything turned out OK, because all four of us have high ethical standards and wouldn't dream of cheating each other. But we had to have a few serious discussions about resolving some issues that came up early in the partnership when we were playing to get back our entry fee. And I could see that this could have been the end of a beautiful friendship if any one of us had been stubborn and inflexible when we needed to change our agreement slightly during early play.

Jamie Gold, the 2006 World Series of Poker main-event winner, and a "partner" weren't so lucky with their oral agreement, which ended up in bitter accusations and a long court struggle. Early in the proceedings, the court released half of the $12 million first prize to Jamie Gold, since that portion had never been in dispute. But the remaining $6 million was held frozen at the Rio casino cage awaiting resolution of the matter through the lawsuits. Fortunately, the two former friends and business associates finally settled out of court, but probably not without a big chunk of the prize money from each man going for lawyer fees.

## FROM RECREATIONAL TO PROFESSIONAL POKER PLAYER

**MARISSA:** In Jean's fourth point at the beginning of this chapter, she suggests that you study Chapter 4 to learn the issues of filing as a recreational or a professional gambler. The considerations for the poker player are pretty much the same as for a gambler in any other game.

If you choose to file as a recreational gambler, you're still required to keep an accurate and complete log of your play. You need to keep your winning-session figures separate from your losing-session ones. When you file, you'll add up all your winning sessions and put that total on Page 1 of the return under "Other Income" (as we did on page 126 in Appendix B1).

If, and only if, you itemize, you can put the total of your losing sessions on Schedule A under "Other Miscellaneous Deductions." See example on page 130 in Appendix B2. Recreational gamblers cannot deduct business expenses.

**JEAN:** What about tips? Time or rake fees? Tournament entry fees? Can a recreational poker player reduce his winnings by these amounts?

**MARISSA:** Tournament entry fees can be totaled with your gambling losses. Time fees also are considered to be part of the win/loss figure, since you're paying them at the table; time fees are analogous to the rake in the smaller cash games.

**JEAN:** But it looks to me like tips are in a gray area. Ordinarily, a recreational player can't deduct tips, which are discretionary. However, it's the longstanding custom at most poker tables to tip the dealer something from each significant pot the player drags. And if you don't do it because it's considered "discretionary," you can suddenly become very unpopular with your fellow players, not to mention the darts shooting from the dealer's eyes.

Because it's almost impossible to keep track of so many tip amounts, some players consider tips just as they do time fees or the rake. They add up all their buy-ins in one session and subtract the amount they cash out, and this is their win or loss figure for their log.

**MARISSA:** Jean has a strong point here, but I'm not sure I could prevail with it in an audit should the IRS, in an unlikely event, question it.

**JEAN:** Filing as a professional poker player, if you find you probably qualify to do so after reading Chapter 4, will have its pros and cons. You'll have to act as though your gambling is a business, with an increase in paperwork, such as detailed records, a separate business bank account, and receipts for expenses. Another con is that you'll have to pay the self-employment tax of about 15%. But the flip side of that is you'll be earning Social Security benefits that might come in handy if you become disabled or want to retire from flipping real or virtual cards.

**MARISSA:** There are many advantages to filing as a professional gambler. One of the biggest is you're able to avoid a large increase in your AGI (adjusted gross income) by not having to use your gross win figure on the front of your 1040. That is a double advantage if you're a resident of a state that taxes you on gross win without any deduction for losses.

Another big plus is the ability to deduct business expenses, which can run high for many poker players. However, I must repeat the warning we put in Chapter 4 for all professional gamblers: Your losses *plus* your expenses may not exceed your winnings.

Below is a list of some expenses a poker player filing as a professional gambler *might* be able to deduct. The IRS states the expense must be "necessary and ordinary." As long as an expense has a predominately (and not tangential) business purpose attached to it, then it may be deducted, within the limits of specific IRS rulings (i.e., 50% of business meals). Basically, any expense needs to pass the "common-sense" test when being considered as to whether or not it may be deducted:

• professional services, such as an accountant, bookkeeper, financial planner, tax preparer, attorney, or the masseuse who gives you massages at the poker table;
• travel expenses, such as hotel, airfare, food, car rental;
• business vehicle expenses;
• home office, including phone and utility expense, supplies, insurance;
• managers' and assistants' salaries, including their commissions and travel expenses;
• tournament entry fees;
• tips;
• professional resources, such as poker books and software, magazine subscriptions, and lessons/seminar fees;
• dues or fees for professional organizations;
• safe-deposit box and banking fees;
• interest on business debt;
• health insurance.

If a poker pro is successful, then he needs to take advantage of all the retirement tax shelters available, like solo 401(k)s and SEP-IRAs.

If a pro is *very* successful (over $300K per year), he can even set up defined benefit plans where he can shelter in excess of $100K per year from taxes.

If a professional poker player also has other revenue streams, such as endorsements, writing, appearance fees, royalties, etc., he may need to consider incorporating. Incorporating has many tax and legal benefits, but each case is unique and you'd need to consult your own tax and/or legal professionals.

As a pro, you'll need a system to keep track of income and expenses. Among the many different ways of doing this, I recommend using QuickBooks or hiring a bookkeeper. Many bookkeepers will come to your house once a month and organize your books. *I've found that those who keep track of their expenses always have the most deductions!*

## NEW POKER TAX RULING—STOP THE PRESSES

**JEAN:** Just before this book went to the printer, the IRS, on September 4, 2007, dropped a bomb on the poker world. They issued Revenue Procedure 2007-57, which states that starting March 8, 2008, there will be a mandatory 25% withholding on all U.S. poker-tournament wins when the money received exceeds the entry and buy-in fees by $5,000. (This ruling affects winnings in casinos and cardrooms in the U.S., but doesn't mention online poker sites or casinos outside the country.)

**MARISSA:** Actually, this is not a brand-new rule. The IRS is just providing clarification of a regulation [Code Sec. 3402(q)(3)(C)(i)] that's already in place, one that has been applied to pari-mutuel horse betting and lotteries for years. They are now putting poker tournaments into the same category, classifying poker as a gambling activity as opposed to being a skillful activity, like Scrabble or chess. (This came as a result of a tax-court ruling that took place earlier this year, stating that tournament poker is not a skillful competition and should be considered a gambling activity, at least for the purposes of taxation.)

This new withholding rule is going to cause a lot of problems within the poker community.

A major problem will be how players, many of whom have "backers," can parcel out this withholding responsibility. One way to resolve the problem is with the use of Form 5754, *Statement by Person(s) Receiving Gambling Winnings*, discussed in Chapter 3. The person who actually wins the tournament fills out Form 5754 with the name(s) and Social Security number(s) of any person(s) sharing in this win and gives it to the casino, which then issues individual W-2Gs based on the information furnished on it. Although it seems that, according to IRS code, a casino is required to accept a Form 5754, in practice most casinos won't honor the form. It will be interesting to see if loud player protests–or even wide tournament boycotts–will make the casinos more amenable to Form 5754 in the future.

**JEAN:** There's no doubt in my mind that this ruling will have a major impact on the "poker economy." The government may say that most people have tax withheld from their paychecks and why should poker winnings be any different? A person's tax liability doesn't change, just the timing of paying some of the tax.

But there are already angry rumblings in gambling forums all over the Internet. Many are pointing out that withholding tax on their winnings ignores the fact that many (most?) players have so many deductions for their losses by the time they file their taxes that they'll pay little or no tax on their wins, certainly not 25%. They say that this 25% interest-free "loan" to the government, in the meantime, will soon put them out of action with a busted bankroll. Most poker players, except for a few in the top echelon who have huge bankrolls, are playing on limited funds. Instead of a player taking the money from one tournament win and playing in another tournament, the IRS gets it. That's one less entry in a tournament. I think you'll see a lot of the mid-range tournaments (with $2,500-$5,000 buy-ins) impacted, since people usually play those tournaments with winnings from previous tournaments.

**MARISSA:** Another interesting consequence of this ruling is that the $1 "free" slot tournament (which we discussed in Chapter 3) might go away. The casino might want to avoid having to withhold the 25% on any prize over $5,001. Therefore, the tournaments might be truly free again. This means, however, that instead of a W-2G, which is unarguably gambling related, you'll get a Form 1099, which the IRS sometimes questions as being part of your gambling income.

What about single-table satellites? At the World Series of Poker when you play a single-table tournament, you win chips that you can't convert to cash; you have to use them to buy into another tournament. I wonder if the IRS will require withholding in that situation. My feeling is that the answer would be "no," since the chips cannot be exchanged for cash.

But this and many other questions will have to be settled down the road. And the ramifications of this new ruling will certainly reverberate through the poker world and change things for years to come.

**JEAN:** Is there any chance that this ruling might be rescinded? I doubt it. Everyone has seen the explosion of poker all over TV and around the world. The IRS isn't blind. They know that there has been a huge under-reporting of wins, due to a very incomplete paperwork trail for poker tournaments. This withholding ruling is a new solid pathway they want to construct. Plus, withholding and making money off the "float" is definitely a technique used by governments to generate revenue without raising taxes. I don't know if that's the intention here, but it's definitely a consequence.

## STOP THE PRESSES, AGAIN

**JEAN:** At the rate we're going, Marissa and I will never get this book to the printer, but we're happy to add this last-minute good news. The IRS listened to the casino industry and withdrew the requirement that casinos withhold 25% of any poker-tournament wins more than $5,000, as we reported in the previous section in this chapter. This relieves the fears of many gamblers that they'll be forced out of tournament action, due to the hit on their bankrolls. And the casinos were saved from the result they feared: that tournament participation would drop off severely.

As with all such negotiations, the IRS did make one new requirement: Casinos must report tournament winnings of more than $5,000 on a W-2G form. Some casinos had been doing this on their own in the past, but now it will be industry wide. This doesn't really change the law for gamblers; gambling winnings have always been taxable and have to be reported whether there's any paperwork issued or not. However, after March 4, 2008, when this new policy takes effect, compliance will be a must for those who haven't been following the law in the past and depending on a totally cash system to stay under the IRS radar.

Now the IRS has the paper trail it wanted!

*"The hardest thing in the world to understand is the income tax."*

—Albert Einstein

# 7
# Audits and Other Scary Tax Problems for the Gambler

**JEAN:** We wish we could tell you that if you read this whole book, you'll always know just how to file your income-tax return, handle your gambling wins and losses, and never have to face an IRS audit. But we can't. All we can do is give you as much information as we know to be the facts of this matter, based on IRS writings and court cases.

However, so much tax information, especially for the gambler, is incomplete, ambiguous, and even contradictory. So much isn't black and white. Therefore, when we enter those vast gray areas, all we can do is talk with careful reservations: likely results, possible options, feasible solutions, and probable outcomes.

Each person's tax situation is unique. This book isn't the tax gospel. To belabor the warning we have given throughout the book: It's paramount that readers of this book get together with their tax professionals if they have any questions about how gambling figures should be treated in their particular circumstances.

With that said, we thought it would be helpful if we used this chapter to spotlight some of the most troublesome tax issues and provide some information that might be useful in dealing with the IRS and in the case of audits.

## "THE IRS ISN'T FAIR"

**JEAN:** I used to tell my children when they were growing up—and I'm repeating this with my grandchildren—that no one ever said life was fair and they might as well get used to it.

Of course, the IRS doesn't accept any blame in the fairness game. They do what government agencies do best: Pass the buck. They would like this quote I found in one court case: "Federal taxes ... rest where Congress has placed them."

I daresay "fair" isn't the adjective most people use when they describe the government, especially the IRS. And that's in spite of the official IRS Mission: "Provide America's taxpayers top-quality service by helping them understand and meet their tax responsibilities and by applying the tax law with integrity and fairness to all."

Is it fair that you can't net out your wins and losses at the end of the year and, therefore, might have a big tax bill in addition to being an overall loser as well? No. It's sad, but it's not fair.

Is it fair that your state won't let you deduct gambling losses so that your state tax bill is higher than the amount you won gambling? Nope. It's not only not fair, but it doesn't make sense either.

Is it fair that a professional gambler can file as a business, but can't write off any gambling losses against other kinds of income, as other businesses do? That's a decidedly unfair double standard!

I wish I could give you a different answer about unfair tax rules, that perhaps things will change for the better in the future. But I see no hope for that, no matter how many e-mails we send our state- and federal-government representatives. In spite of the broad spread of casinos all over our country and the seemingly wider acceptance of gambling, it's still viewed as a moral issue by enough people that most politicians are afraid to go on record in favor of it. In fact, so many of them are quick to support sin taxes that there's more likelihood that tax rules on gambling will become more restrictive, rather than loosening up, in the future.

# THE 1040 LINE 21 PROBLEM

**JEAN:** Perhaps one of the biggest problems facing gamblers is the issue of how to report gambling wins and losses on a tax return. In Chapter 4, we talked about the professional gambler and how he can use Schedule C to net out his gambling wins and losses so he doesn't have to worry about Line 21 on his 1040. But most gamblers file as recreational players and have to decide what gambling win figure to put on line 21, Other Income.

Back in Chapter 4, we agreed that the IRS clearly states that you should keep your wins and losses separate. That seems like they're talking about winning and losing "sessions," but as we've seen, the IRS doesn't define what a session is. So we discussed how sessions might be of various lengths depending on many individual factors in your particular circumstances, e.g., what game you played. But we decided a session logically would be a group of hands, not a separate one for each individual hand. The latter would make for next-to-impossible record-keeping.

So for years, many players, at the suggestion of their tax preparers, added up all their winning sessions of the year and put that total, labeled "Gambling Income," on line 21, Other Income, of their 1040 forms. They were careful to attach a sheet to their return that listed all their W-2Gs and gambling-related 1099s with a note that these were all accounted for in the total they put on Line 21. If they chose to itemize, they listed the total session losses as a deduction on Schedule A. Evidently, the IRS was usually happy with handling one's gambling action in this way, because most players were never audited or even questioned about this.

However, within the last couple of years, the IRS, although they never changed their written instructions or rules about the matter, has begun to more frequently question this procedure on some gamblers' returns. Why this change?

It's impossible to figure out the collective mind of the IRS, but I'm guessing it's the result of a new push in the last few years to encourage better tax compliance in the fast-growing gambling arena. Cash operations are always a fertile field in which to find new sources of unreported income.

So what's the reporting procedure the IRS seems to like now, at least in some cases, instead of session totals? They've instructed some taxpayers to enter the total of all of their W-2Gs as their "Gambling Income" on line 21, even though this figure is nothing like the records the IRS demands in a gaming log. In reality, a W-2G jackpot is just the result of one hand.

Why would the IRS do such an illogical thing? All gamblers know that they have some days when they win, although they don't get any paperwork. In fact, in past audits, the IRS wouldn't accept records that showed only W-2G wins; they know you have others. On the other hand, gamblers who get W-2Gs know painfully well that they don't take home all their W-2G jackpots. In fact, in some sessions, you end up losing even if you have multiple W-2Gs.

**MARISSA:** The main reason for this problem is that right now, the only way that the IRS computers "check" as to whether or not you're reporting your gambling winnings is through the use of the W-2G, even though this is a highly inaccurate measure of your actual winnings. You're playing a $10 Jacks or Better video poker machine. You get lucky at first and hit two quads, and you're issued two W-2Gs for $1,250 each. Then, before you know it, you hit a dry spell, lose all the money back, and walk away even. The problem is that although you're even for your gambling session, the IRS has on file that you won $2,500.

The W-2G threshold of $1,200 is far too low vis-à-vis the denominations and kinds of games that are available these days. When the rules were created 30 or so years ago, there was no such thing as multi-line video poker and single-play dollar machines were considered high-roller games. If you hit a slot machine for $1,200, you probably were ahead for the day, week, month, and maybe even the year. With single line, 3-coin, very slow machines, it was hard to pump a lot of money through. Today, running $10,000 an hour through a quick machine isn't unusual. Essentially, you now have a situation where current conditions and archaic thresholds are colliding.

**JEAN:** Not every gambler will have a problem here. If your session wins add up to more than your W-2G total, the computer won't kick out your return, and if a live IRS employee sees this figure, he'll think you're very lucky—or crazy and super-honest.

**MARISSA:** If your W-2G total amount is not much larger than your actual session win, I'd understand your trying to avoid a possible IRS hassle by using the W-2G figure, even if you have to pay a little more in taxes.

For some players, however, this option isn't feasible. In Chapter 4, we listed a number of negative factors that would come into play on a federal return. And in Chapter 8, we discuss how gamblers in some states would also be seriously impacted. If they have a much larger W-2G amount than their gross win amount done by sessions, it might be cheaper for them to pay for professional advice and/or representation (if they're audited) than to pay a much larger tax bill and/or lose deductions because of a larger AGI (adjusted gross income) figure. And for those in states where there's an income tax on wins, but no allowance for losses, a large AGI can be extremely costly.

The good news is that taxpayers usually resolve this problem with the IRS with positive results. The bad news is that this takes time, usually 12-18 months, writing back and forth and working through the levels of the IRS. I've personally been involved in many of these kinds of cases and most get resolved within two or three rounds of letters. I've had two cases filed and ready to go to tax court, only to have them settled at the pre-trial conference.

In summary, reporting a number that's less than your W-2G total is controversial, even among tax professionals, and untested in the courts. Until there are clear instructions from the IRS, as well as definitive court cases, this must be decided on a case-by-case basis and depends on the willingness of the gambler to fight the IRS.

**JEAN:** In December 2008, the IRS put out a Technical Advice Memorandum of special interest to gamblers; it concerned "Reporting of Wagering Gains and Losses," with this burning issue: *How does a casual gambler determine wagering gains and losses from slot machine play?*

This memo, which you can read at www.irs.gov/pub/irs-utl/am2008011.pdf, seems to legitimize what Marissa and I discuss about using the session method in reporting gambling wins and losses: ... *A casual gambler, such as the taxpayer who plays the slot machines, recognizes a wagering gain or loss at the time she redeems her tokens. We think that the fluctuating wins and losses left in play are not accessions to wealth until the taxpayer redeems her tokens and can definitively calculate the amount above or below basis (the wager) realized.*

A footnote in this memo directly contradicts the all-too-common practice of the IRS disputing the return of a gambler who doesn't use the W-2G amount as his "wins": *We note that § 6041 requires gambling businesses to report payments over certain dollar amounts, "gross receipts" reporting. The amount reported as gross receipts from many types of gambling is not reduced by the amount (basis) of the wager. See Rev. Proc. 77-29, 1977-2 C.B. 538. However, such reported payments are not necessarily taxable wagering gains. A gambling business may issue an information return for a casual gambler's winning spin, but the gambler continues play and wagers and loses that amount during slot machine play. Wagering gain or loss is determined at the time the casual gambler redeems his or her tokens at the end of slot machine play.*

This memo does include an admonition: *This advice may not be used or cited as precedent.* However, I have already referred to this memo with good results when helping a friend with a letter audit disputing his using the session method. The response from the IRS was quick and happiness-producing: "You don't owe us $80,000 after all!"

Marissa hopes that this memo will be the start of an IRS trend toward a better understanding of gambling issues and thinks it can probably be used when dealing with the IRS at the administrative levels.

## GETTING INFORMATION FROM AN IRS HUMAN

**JEAN:** In the beginning of this chapter, I talked about the writings of the IRS as being incomplete, ambiguous, and even contradictory. I can use those same adjectives about information you might get from a live IRS employee. It's almost a cliché that you can get 10 different opinions about a tax issue if you talk to 10 different IRS staffers. So my first piece of advice about getting information on tax questions about gambling is not to depend on the word of only one IRS employee.

**MARISSA:** This is especially important if you call a general IRS hotline. Most of the customer-service representatives answering these phones are entry-level workers who have sparse knowledge about the nuances of gambling. Revenue agents who are entry-level auditors usually aren't much better informed, since this isn't an issue they deal with frequently, especially those who live outside of Nevada. Revenue agents are usually junior or entry-level positions filled with individuals fresh out of college with a four-year accounting degree, but no experience with gambling numbers. Revenue officers are a little more senior and some of them do understand gambling issues. (Occasionally, you might get lucky and find a supervisor or a manager at these units who understands gambling today as it relates to gambling law.) You'll usually have your best luck with those people within the IRS who gamble themselves. They can usually understand what you're trying to ask or convey to them.

Once you've found an IRS person whose advice seems to make sense and you plan to use it, it's very important to get his IRS employee badge number. If he gives you erroneous advice, you rely upon that advice, and it later turns out to be incorrect, then you're not liable for penalties and interest. Worst case, you'll only have to pay the tax you would have had to pay in the first place if you'd received correct information.

## SURVIVING AN AUDIT

**JEAN:** A simple white envelope from the IRS can strike terror in almost anyone. And one of the most dreaded phrases in the English language is "tax audit." A survey once found that people would rather have major surgery than go through an IRS audit.

True, no IRS audit is fun. And there's no *sure* way to avoid one. The IRS doesn't publish a list of things on a tax return that can trigger an audit.

However, IRS Publication 556, *Examination of Returns, Appeal Rights, and Claims for Refund,* does shed some general light on the matter: *If your return is selected for examination, it does not suggest that you made an error or are dishonest. Returns are chosen by computerized screening, by random sample, or by an income document matching program.* (I love it that the IRS likes to refer to audits as "examinations." That sounds so much friendlier!)

**MARISSA:** Most audits that result from computerized screening aren't due to just one "red flag." Yes, a cash operation can raise your odds of an audit, as can a home office, amending your return, and being self-employed or owning a small business. These last two have been special targets of the IRS in recent years, so a professional gambler needs to be prepared with very detailed and accurate records. If a casino files a CTR (Currency Transaction Report) or a SAR (Suspicious Activity Report) on you, that definitely increases your audit "score." Going to Publication 556 again: *A computer program called the Discriminate Inventory Function System (DIF) assigns a numeric score to each individual and some corporate tax returns after they have been processed. If your return is selected because of a high score under the DIF system, the potential is high that examination of your return will result in a change to your income tax liability.* It's your total score that triggers the audit, the big picture of your personal circumstances. A high-enough DIF means your return gets kicked to a human, and in some situations, a human ultimately decides whether you get audited.

**JEAN:** Many audits are triggered because of the IRS' "income document matching program." These are sent out automatically by computers and often haven't been seen by human eyes. In Chapter 5 we talked about these CP-2000 letters, sometimes referred to as "letter audits." Sometimes one letter of explanation to the IRS can resolve these, especially if it seems to be a simple mistake, such as an attachment to your original return that has been lost or overlooked. This is a common situation. Often, sending a copy of the original attachment with your explanation solves the problem.

If you paid someone to do your taxes, it's wise to get his/her advice about the proper response to any letter from the IRS. In fact, I recommend that you check with a professional tax preparer in any case. If you write the letter yourself, it's very important to keep this first response very simple. The temptation is to "explain" too much. One poster in an Internet forum discussion on taxes put it nicely: "What happens when you send too much information is that the IRS ends up asking more questions based on the extra information—hoist by his own petard is the expression that comes to mind."

A former "letter audit grunt," as he called himself, added good advice to this same Internet forum discussion: "Letter audits are usually entry-level tasks for future auditors. They're generally on some point(s) not deemed major enough for a full-blown office audit. Not only are the grunts looking for some simple explanation, but anything too complicated is likely to scare them into thinking, 'Wow! Must be serious,' and automatically kicking it up to the next IRS level. Keep it as simple as possible. The letters at this stage aren't seen by anyone other than grunts. Make it easy for them to understand. Absolutely not the time or place to write an amateur legal document citing cases."

It was recommended in this same forum discussion that you send your response to an audit letter back to the IRS by certified mail with a return receipt requested. "The IRS is noted for losing things!"

**MARISSA:** If your first response to an IRS audit letter doesn't resolve the issue to your satisfaction, your next step is deciding whether you have the tenacity to continue what might be a long battle. Some gamblers have decided it's less hassle and cheaper in the long run to pay what the IRS insists that they owe, concede the victory to the IRS, and leave the field. Others dig in for the long haul.

Although some individuals have the ability to do the research and write the letters and the patience to continue the battle, most wisely turn the problem over to a tax professional. It helps them with your case if you've kept a detailed gambling log and collected supporting evidence of your gambling action. The more records you have, the more likely it is that you'll win in an audit.

If your case isn't resolved with letters, a face-to-face meeting with an IRS agent will be necessary. You can do this scary activity alone, but most feel more comfortable having a tax professional with them or sending them as your representative and not appearing at all. This latter choice is often the best one. Not surprisingly, taxpayers are usually very nervous during an audit and, therefore, tend to—just as in their letters to the IRS—try to convince by giving too many unrelated details, which may open more dangerous lines of questioning.

Not all audits resolve the gambler's problem to his satisfaction. However, remember this: If you filed your return in good faith, with no intent to fraudulently misrepresent the facts, the worst that will happen if you don't prevail in an audit (or a subsequent tax-court appearance if you take your fight that far) is that you'll be assessed additional taxes and interest (and perhaps some late penalties, which can sometimes be negotiated down).

**JEAN:** And perhaps you'll eventually be able to look at things on the sunny side, as did this poster on the Internet-forum tax discussion we've been mentioning: "You should try to relax a little about the whole matter of IRS audits. Yes, you might have to pay more taxes. But you won't go to jail unless they can prove you tried to defraud the government. A tax audit isn't fun, but if you've been honest, it's not criminal. It's just about the money."

But then again, you may never be this relaxed!

# THE TAXPAYER ADVOCATE

The Taxpayer Advocate Service is one that is not widely known. This is the IRS description of the program and how it can help you with tax problems. The following is a brief version of this service:

Where do you go when the IRS representatives who are auditing or processing your return do not seem to understand your problems or situation? One place is the IRS Taxpayer Advocate Service. Its motto is: "We help taxpayers solve problems with the IRS and recommend changes that will prevent them."

The Taxpayer Advocate Service is an IRS program that provides an independent system to assure that tax problems that have not been resolved through normal channels are promptly and fairly handled. The national taxpayer advocate, Nina Olson, heads the program. Each state and service center has at least one local taxpayer advocate who is independent of the local IRS office and reports directly to the national taxpayer advocate. The goals of the Taxpayer Advocate Service are to protect individual taxpayer rights and reduce taxpayer burden. The taxpayer advocate independently represents your interests and concerns within the IRS. This is accomplished in two ways:

• ensuring that taxpayer problems that have not been resolved through normal channels are promptly and fairly handled;
• identifying issues that increase the burden upon or create problems for taxpayers, and bringing those issues to the attention of IRS management and making legislative proposals when necessary.

What can you expect from the taxpayer advocate? Your assigned personal advocate will listen to your point of view and will work with you to address your concerns.

You can expect the advocate to provide you with the following:

• a "fresh look" at your problem

- timely acknowledgment
- the name and phone number of the individual assigned to your case
- updates on progress
- time frames for action
- speedy resolution
- courteous service

Who may use the Taxpayer Advocate Service? Generally, the Taxpayer Advocate Service can help if, as a result of the application of the tax laws, you:

- are suffering, or are about to suffer, a significant hardship;
- are facing an immediate threat of adverse action;
- will incur significant cost (including fees for professional representation);
- will suffer irreparable injury or long-term adverse impact;
- have experienced a delay of more than 30 days to resolve an issue; or
- have not received a response or resolution by the date promised.

If you have an ongoing issue with the IRS that has not been resolved through normal processes, or you have suffered or are about to suffer a significant hardship as a result of the application of the tax laws, contact the Taxpayer Advocate Service.

Note: The Taxpayer Advocate Service is not a substitute for established IRS procedures or the formal appeals process. The Taxpayer Advocate Service cannot reverse legal or technical tax determinations.

So, how do you reach the Taxpayer Advocate Service? Call the Taxpayer Advocate Service toll-free telephone number: 877/777-4778. Call the general IRS toll-free number, 800/829-1040, and request the Taxpayer Advocate Service. Call, write, or visit the local Taxpayer Advocate Service office for your state. A list of Taxpayer

Advocate Service offices may be found in Publication 1546, *The Taxpayer Advocate Service of the IRS*.

Complete and submit Form 911, *Application for Taxpayer Assistance Order*. You should provide the following information:

- your name, address, and social security number (or employer identification number);
- your telephone number and hours you can be reached;
- your previous attempts to solve the problem, and the office you contacted;
- the type of tax return and year(s) involved;
- description of the problem or hardship (if applicable).

If you want to authorize another person to discuss the matter or to receive information about your case, use Form 2848, *Power of Attorney and Declaration of Representative*. You may also want to use Form 2848 *Instructions*. Or, you may use Form 8821, *Tax Information Authorization*, if you want another person to receive information about your case but not represent you. You can get these forms at most local IRS offices or by calling the IRS forms-only number.

# Part II

# State Taxes

*"Another difference between death and taxes is that death is frequently painless."*

—Anonymous

# 8
# States Add Insult to Injury

**JEAN:** If you're a gambler, you're lucky if you reside in one of the six tax-haven (or tax-heaven, in my opinion) states that don't have any form of state income tax (Washington, Nevada, Texas, Alaska, South Dakota, and Wyoming). This is also true if you live in the near tax-haven states, like Florida, which only tax intangibles, or in Tennessee or New Hampshire, which only tax investments. Why are you lucky? You won't have to pay your state any taxes on your gambling wins.

## STATE WITHHOLDING TAXES

However, you're not completely safe from *all* state income taxes. You may gamble and hit a jackpot in another state, one that *does* have a state income tax, a few of which *automatically* withhold state taxes from any win that generates a federal W-2G, regardless of the residency of the jackpot winner. This list of the latter (and the percentage that they withhold) includes:

- Louisiana: 6%
- Iowa: 5%
- Missouri: 4%
- Indiana: 3.4%
- Mississippi: 3% (The tax is withheld for all W-2G wins, but this is what they call a non-refundable state income tax—see further explanation in this chapter.)
- Michigan: 4.35% (This withholding is for non-residents only and covers winnings from casinos, racetracks, and off-track betting.)
- Connecticut: 5% (No withholding for anyone unless federal withholding is required, i.e., non-resident aliens.)

If you're a resident of one of the first four states in the above list and hit a jackpot on which the casinos in your own state withhold state income taxes, you don't have a problem with this, since you'll be paying state income taxes anyway and you can easily file for a refund if the amount withheld is more than your tax obligation.

However, if you live in Louisiana, Indiana, Michigan, or Connecticut, you face the same huge problem that residents in many other states face: the inability to deduct gambling losses from gambling wins. We talk about that problem later in this chapter. And the tax situation in Mississippi is so confusing that we give that state a whole section to itself.

## TAXES ON NON-RESIDENT GAMING

**JEAN:** Once a non-resident has state income tax withheld on a gambling jackpot, it becomes a tax problem that can be very complex, depending on the two states involved and each of their tax rules and regulations. Each state has its own way of calculating income taxes for non-residents and for handling out-of-state income. Some states have reciprocity agreements with neighboring states or allow a credit on their own state form for taxes paid to other states, thereby alleviating the hassle of filing two state tax returns or being double-taxed. In any case, be sure to attach necessary documentation (like W-2Gs or 1099s or other state returns) to show where taxes from other states have been withheld or paid.

However, in many cases it's a royal pain! If you're entitled to a total or partial refund (and you aren't in all cases), you may have to file a non-resident state form for the state where the jackpot was hit. I had to do this several years ago when I was an Indiana resident, hit a W-2G jackpot in Mississippi, and had 5% withheld for the Mississippi state income tax (they have since changed their system as I explain in a later section). It was a nightmare in Fraction Land, since all Mississippi figures had to be reported as a percentage of my federal figures.

Many gamblers just don't bother filing a non-resident return to get a refund, especially a small one. And this might actually wind up being cheaper in the long run, especially if a professional has to be paid to do the extra tax return.

**MARISSA:** You may wonder if you need to file a non-resident state return in the case of a win in another state where no state tax is withheld. If you win money in another state that has a state income tax, you're technically supposed to file a return in that state. However, in practice, very few do.

In the past, some states vigorously pursued out-of-state winners. California used to track down non-resident racetrack winners and bill them for California state taxes. In the early '90s, New Jersey chased non-resident jackpot winners for a while, but then dropped the idea. Legally, any state can pursue out-of-state winners. However, this is difficult, because of widespread ignorance of state laws by non-resident taxpayers or deliberate non-compliance with them. As you can see by the above list, the trend is for the state to take the easier route and withhold taxes on the spot from all W-2G winnings or, in Michigan's case, all non-resident jackpots. I won't be surprised to see more and more of them doing this in the near future.

As we've repeated numerous times in this book, you need to check with a tax professional to get up-to-date tax information. This is especially crucial with state tax matters. I foresee a lot of new state gambling-tax legislation in the future, since there's a strong trend for states to consider casinos their cash cows.

## THE BIGGEST PROBLEM WITH STATE TAXATION

**JEAN:** Some states allow deductions for gross gambling losses to offset gross wins on their state returns, just as the feds do if you itemize. However, one of the biggest problems for many gamblers is in those states that base their income taxes on the federal adjusted gross income (AGI) figure, which includes the gross-win figure, while the state form has no allowance for gambling losses.

Our former state of residence, Indiana, is an example (see Appendix B4 for an Indiana sample tax form). Before we started filing as a business, which allowed us to net out our winnings, we complained about the unusual pain of having too many winning sessions! This unfair situation has made many a taxpayer give up gambling entirely, since he's almost certain to lose in the tax game even if he wins at the casino game. And others have actually moved to more tax-friendly states, so they can continue with their chosen vocation or avocation of gambling.

A note: You may have *triple* tax trouble if you not only live in a state that has an income tax, but live in a city that has a municipal income tax as well. Each city has its own ordinances about how to treat gambling action. My only advice is to seek professional tax help in sorting through all the tax issues you'll have.

**MARISSA:** For states that have an income tax, there are just a few main ways in which they treat gambling wins and losses. The majority of states "follow the federal." That is, the format of the state returns is similar to the federal tax return, including permitting the deduction of gambling losses against gambling winnings.

Some states are what we in the business call "above the line"—states that follow the federal tax return only as far as the AGI (adjusted gross income) line. The key point here is that these states *do not* allow itemized deductions; therefore, since gambling losses are an itemized deduction on the federal form, there's no place for them on the state forms (or they have special instructions that effectively bring the same result).

The following above-the-line states make it almost impossible to gamble with an advantage, no matter how skilled you are, and many recreational gamblers can't gamble as much as they'd like because of the severe tax bite:

Connecticut
Illinois
Indiana
Louisiana
Massachusetts
Michigan
Ohio
Oregon
West Virginia
Wisconsin

Two states, New Jersey and Pennsylvania, allow the taxpayer to net gambling wins and losses before reporting. It's too bad that other states, and the federal government, don't follow their example!

## MISSISSIPPI—A CATEGORY OF ITS OWN

**JEAN:** Finally, there's Mississippi, which adds a new kink to state income taxes on gambling. Formerly, they automatically withheld 5% state income tax from W-2G jackpots, but in 2002 they began taking out a non-refundable 3% gaming tax. For a couple of years, no one really knew what to call it. Was it a gambling tax? Was it a sin tax, similar to the one on cigarettes? Finally, the state, in the instructions for their state tax forms, began calling it a non-refundable state income tax.

**MARISSA:** Mississippi residents do get a small break, wherein the W-2G amount doesn't have to be counted in their gross income for state income-tax purposes. And non-residents who live in a state with an income tax may take the withheld Mississippi tax as a credit on their state taxes if they've counted Mississippi winnings in their gambling income. Or those who itemize on their federal return could list the withheld amount as a deduction on Schedule A, under State Income Taxes. It is, however, a preference item for figuring the Alternative Minimum Tax, which means that the deduction could hurt you in certain situations. Gamblers who file as professionals may take this Mississippi withholding as a business expense.

**JEAN:** If I still lived in Indiana and hit a W-2G jackpot as I did before this new law went into effect, I wouldn't need to go through the hassle I described earlier of filing a non-resident Mississippi state return. I could simply take the amount of the Mississippi tax withheld as a credit against my Indiana state taxes. Since I now live in Nevada, which has no state tax, and I file as a business, if I have Mississippi tax withheld, I can list that amount as a business expense.

## ANY RELIEF FROM STATE TAXES?

**JEAN:** We mentioned earlier that some people actually quit gambling or move to a more tax-friendly state in order to escape the burden of unreasonable state taxation. Is there another option?

There's one for a few gamblers: filing as a professional. Being able to deduct expenses and net out your wins and losses on Schedule C of your federal return allows you to report on your state return a realistic net income, rather than the much larger figure representing your gross wins.

However, it required more than half of Chapter 4 to discuss the stiff requirements for filing as a professional gambler. Our constant reminder to seek professional tax help is especially germane here. Filing as a professional may put you on a very bumpy road with the IRS as your too-close companion. And many people have found states to be very tough, even if you finally convince the feds. As I write this, I'm involved as an expert witness in a Michigan tax case against a video poker player. Even though the IRS has given its approval to her filing as a professional gambler, the state is arguing against that status on her state return.

In the next chapter is a state-by-state list with summary information on individual states and how they treat gambling income and losses. Notice that many states have special rules about lottery wins. This list is up to date as of the summer of 2007, but we suggest that you use the Internet to keep up with changes in state income tax laws.

*"A fine is a tax for doing something wrong. A tax is a fine for doing something right."*

—Anonymous

# How All 50 States Handle Gambling Wins/Losses

**ALABAMA:** Follows federal law as it pertains to gambling winnings and losses.

**ALASKA:** No state income tax.

**ARIZONA:** Follows federal law, except for Arizona Lottery winnings and losses.

**ARKANSAS:** Follows federal law as it pertains to gambling winnings and losses.

**CALIFORNIA:** Follows federal law as it pertains to gambling winnings and losses, except for California Lottery winnings and losses.

**COLORADO:** Follows federal law as it pertains to gambling winnings and losses.

**CONNECTICUT:** No deduction for gambling losses (out-of-state residents are exempt from Connecticut taxes on gambling winnings there, but in-state residents are not). No automatic withholding of state taxes for anyone unless federal withholding is required, i.e., non-resident aliens. However, you may request that the casino withhold federal and/or state taxes (5%).

**DELAWARE:** Follows federal law as it pertains to gambling winnings and losses, except for Delaware Lottery winnings and losses.

**DISTRICT OF COLUMBIA:** Follows federal law as it pertains to gambling winnings and losses.

**FLORIDA:** Does not tax gambling income.

**GEORGIA:** Follows federal law as it pertains to gambling winnings and losses.

**HAWAII:** Follows federal law as it pertains to gambling winnings and losses.

**IDAHO:** Follows federal law as it pertains to gambling winnings and losses, except for Idaho Lottery winnings and losses.

**ILLINOIS:** No deduction for gambling losses. Some casinos will withhold state taxes if you request it.

**INDIANA:** No deduction for gambling losses. Subtraction allowed for Indiana Lottery winnings. (See Appendix B4 for sample Indiana tax forms.) Some casinos treat poker tournament wins just like machine jackpots and issue a W-2G and withhold 3.4% state income tax for any amount of $1,200 and above.

**IOWA:** Follows federal law as it pertains to gambling winnings and losses.

**KANSAS:** Follows federal law as it pertains to gambling winnings and losses.

**KENTUCKY:** Follows federal law as it pertains to gambling winnings and losses.

**LOUISIANA:** No deduction allowed for gambling losses. Minimum 2.4% state tax on wins.

**MAINE:** Follows federal law as it pertains to gambling winnings and losses.

**MARYLAND:** Follows federal law as it pertains to gambling winnings and losses.

**MASSACHUSETTS:** No deduction allowed for gambling losses, except for the cost of the wager on gambling winnings.

**MICHIGAN:** No deduction allowed for gambling losses. *"Michigan withholding is required on all reportable winnings by non-residents at Michigan casinos, racetracks, or off-track betting facilities. Reportable winnings are those winnings required to be reported to the Internal Revenue Service (IRS) under the Internal Revenue Code."*

**MINNESOTA:** Follows federal law as it pertains to gambling winnings and losses.

**MISSISSIPPI:** Follows federal law as it pertains to gambling winnings and losses, except—for Mississippi residents—winnings from Mississippi gaming establishments are *not* included in gambling winnings and losses from Mississippi gaming establishments are *not* included in gambling losses. State tax withheld from winnings from Mississippi gaming establishments is not refundable. In the instructions for their state tax forms, they call it a *non-refundable state income tax.*

**MISSOURI:** Follows federal law as it pertains to gambling winnings and losses.

**MONTANA:** Follows federal law as it pertains to gambling winnings and losses.

**NEBRASKA:** Follows federal law as it pertains to gambling winnings and losses.

**NEVADA:** No state income tax.

**NEW HAMPSHIRE:** Does not tax gambling income.

**NEW JERSEY:** Net gambling winnings are reported on line 23 of NJ-1040. New Jersey Lottery winnings are not taxable; New Jersey Lottery losses are not deductible.

**NEW MEXICO:** Follows federal law as it pertains to gambling winnings and losses.

**NEW YORK:** Follows federal law as it pertains to gambling winnings and losses.

**NORTH CAROLINA:** Follows federal law as it pertains to gambling winnings and losses.

**NORTH DAKOTA:** Follows federal law as it pertains to gambling winnings and losses.

**OHIO:** No deduction allowed for gambling losses.

**OKLAHOMA:** Follows federal law as it pertains to gambling winnings and losses.

**OREGON:** Gambling losses from federal Schedule A must be added back as income on Oregon tax return.

**PENNSYLVANIA:** Net gambling winnings are reported on line 8 of PA-40. Pennsylvania Lottery winnings are not taxable; Pennsylvania Lottery losses are not deductible.

**RHODE ISLAND:** Follows federal law as it pertains to gambling winnings and losses.

**SOUTH CAROLINA:** Follows federal law as it pertains to gambling winnings and losses.

**SOUTH DAKOTA:** No state income tax.

**TENNESSEE:** Does not tax gambling income.

**TEXAS:** No state income tax.

**UTAH:** Follows federal law as it pertains to gambling winnings and losses.

**VERMONT:** Follows federal law as it pertains to gambling winnings and losses.

**VIRGINIA:** Follows federal law as it pertains to gambling winnings and losses.

**WASHINGTON:** No state income tax.

**WEST VIRGINIA:** No deduction allowed for gambling losses.

**WISCONSIN:** No deduction allowed for gambling losses.

**WYOMING:** No state income tax.

*"I'm proud to be paying taxes in the United States. The only thing is, I could be just as proud for half the money."*

—Arthur Godfrey

# Summary

**JEAN:** Marissa and I didn't write this book with the purpose of scaring you, although federal and state taxes can be a frightening matter. Rather, we wrote it with the purpose of helping you become better informed so you might avoid possible tax problems in the future. You must remember the disclaimers and warnings we gave earlier: Every person's tax situation is unique; no one set of rules fits all. This is the reason why we pound home the necessity of getting expert/professional guidance in this area.

You must remember that your gambling figures will be viewed by the IRS as part of your total financial picture. Figures that would be unbelievable for a person with a modest income living an extravagant lifestyle could be very believable for a highly paid executive.

**MARISSA:** Despite common belief, the IRS wants to get to the "truth," not summarily disallow deductions. They will evaluate your gambling figures in the grand scheme of your whole life.

**JEAN:** The following quote comes directly from an IRS publication that gives guidance on that all-important subject of gambling record-keeping: *These record-keeping suggestions are intended as general guidelines to help you establish your winnings and losses. They are not all-inclusive.* *YOUR TAX LIABILITY DEPENDS ON YOUR PARTIC-ULAR FACTS AND CIRCUMSTANCES* (emphasis added).

The biggest problem I faced early on while gathering information was the widely varying opinions of the professionals and the resources I consulted, from the very conservative to the extremely aggressive. Therefore, my final piece of advice to you, my dear reader, on a subject that is so much more gray than black and white, would have to be the same advice I give myself when I'm faced with any wilderness of maze-like paths and puzzling signs: Let conscience and good sense be your guide.

## WHO'S WHO IN THE TAX BUSINESS

**JEAN:** Although any tax preparer can go along with you to an audit for clarification purposes, only three categories of tax professionals can represent you and advocate for you (with or without your presence) before the IRS: certified public accountants (CPAs), attorneys, and enrolled agents (EAs).

CPAs typically have a minimum of four years of college, while attorneys have a minimum of seven years of higher education. They're both licensed by the state and may or may not specialize in taxes.

Enrolled Agents are licensed by the federal government and always specialize in taxes. They qualify by passing an exam covering all aspects of taxation or by having been an IRS employee for five years in a position where they dealt with the IRS code and regulations. They're required to take 72 hours of continuing professional education every three years to maintain their status.

**MARISSA:** I can't emphasize it strongly enough: On the subject of taxes, you always need to check the most current edition of any book and consult a professional who keeps up to date on all the latest tax changes.

And remember, any tax professional who publishes anything on taxes will have a tendency, in gray areas, to take a conservative stance in interpreting the tax codes and regulations in print. Their sword of Damocles is that the IRS has the statutory authority, although seldom used, to unilaterally bar them from practice.

## USEFUL WEBSITES

Internal Revenue Service—www.irs.gov
Links to state tax forms—www.taxadmin.org
Court case resource—www.ustaxcourt.gov
US tax code online—www.fourmilab.ch/uscode/26usc/
Links to tax information—www.el.com/links/taxes.html
American Institute of Certified Public Accountants—
www.aicpa.org
National Association of Enrolled Agents—www.naea.org
National Association of Tax Preparers—www.natptax.com
Website of Professor I. Nelson Rose—
www.gamblingandthelaw.com/
Website of lawyer Chuck Humphrey—
www.gambling-law-us.com/
Information about filing as a professional gambler—
www.professionalgamblerstatus.com/

Be warned that the information you find on private "unofficial" websites may be just one person's opinion and/or interpretation. Even the information found on the official IRS site is often unclear and open to various interpretations, even by IRS employees.

# Casino-Issued Forms

## Appendix A1
## Certain Gambling Winnings

## W-2G

| | | |
|---|---|---|
| ☐ CORRECTED | | |

| PAYER'S name, address, ZIP code, federal identification number, and telephone number | 1 Gross winnings | 2 Federal income tax withheld | OMB No. 1545-0238 |
|---|---|---|---|
| **Palms Hotel and Casino** | 4000 | 0 | 20**07** |
| 4231 W Flamingo Road | 3 Type of wager **SLOTS** | 4 Date won 12 ¦ 1 ¦ 2007 | Form W-2G |
| | 5 Transaction | 6 Race | Certain Gambling Winnings |
| Las Vegas, NV 89102 | 7 Winnings from identical wagers | 8 Cashier | |
| WINNER'S name, address (including apt. no.), and ZIP code **Jean Scott** | 9 Winner's taxpayer identification no. 123456789 | 10 Window | |
| | 11 First I.D. | 12 Second I.D. | |
| 123 Main Street | 13 State/Payer's state identification no. | 14 State income tax withheld | Copy 1 For State Tax Department |
| Las Vegas NV 89102 | | | |

Under penalties of perjury, I declare that, to the best of my knowledge and belief, the name, address, and taxpayer identification number that I have furnished correctly identify me as the recipient of this payment and any payments from identical wagers, and that no other person is entitled to any part of these payments.

Signature ►                           Date ►

Form **W-2G**                  Department of the Treasury - Internal Revenue Service

## W-2G (Instructions to Winner)

### Instructions to Winner

**Box 1.** The payer must furnish a Form W-2G to you if you receive:

1. $600 or more in gambling winnings and the payout is at least 300 times the amount of the wager (except winnings from bingo, keno, and slot machines);

2. $1,200 or more in gambling winnings from bingo or slot machines;

3. $1,500 or more in proceeds (the amount of winnings less the amount of the wager) from keno; or

4. Any gambling winnings subject to federal income tax withholding.

Generally, report all gambling winnings on the "Other income" line of Form 1040. You can deduct gambling losses as an itemized deduction, but you cannot deduct more than your winnings. Keep an accurate record of your winnings and losses, and be able to prove those amounts with receipts, tickets, statements, or similar items that you have saved. For additional information, see Pub. 17, Your Federal Income Tax, Pub. 505, Tax Withholding and Estimated Tax, and Pub. 525, Taxable and Nontaxable Income.

**Box 2.** Any federal income tax withheld on these winnings is shown in this box. Federal income tax must be withheld at the rate of 25% on certain winnings less the wager.

If you did not provide your federal identification number to the payer, the amount in this box may be subject to backup withholding at a 28% rate.

Include the amount shown in box 2 on your Form 1040 as federal income tax withheld.

**Signature.** You must sign Form W-2G if you are the only person entitled to the winnings and the winnings are subject to regular gambling withholding.

**Other winners.** Prepare Form 5754, Statement by Person(s) Receiving Gambling Winnings, if another person is entitled to any part of these winnings. Give Form 5754 to the payer.

## Appendix A1-continued

# W-2G (Instructions for Payers)

### Instructions for Payers

General and specific form instructions are provided as separate products. The products you should use to complete Form W-2G are the 2007 General Instructions for Forms 1099, 1098, 5498, and W-2G and the 2007 Instructions for Forms W-2G and 5754. To order these instructions and additional forms, visit the IRS website at *www.irs.gov,* or call 1-800-TAX-FORM (1-800-829-3676).

**Due dates.** Furnish Copies B and C of this form to the winner by January 31, 2008.

File Copy A of this form with the IRS by February 28, 2008. If you file electronically, the due date is March 31, 2008.

**Gambling withholding.** You may be required to withhold federal income tax from cash or noncash gambling winnings. See the 2007 Instructions for Forms W-2G and 5754 for the rates.

**Foreign winners.** Use Form 1042-S, Foreign Person's U.S. Source Income Subject to Withholding, to report gambling winnings paid to nonresident aliens and foreign corporations. See the Instructions for Form 1042-S. You may be required to withhold federal income tax at a 30% rate. See Pub. 515, Withholding of Tax on Nonresident Aliens and Foreign Entities.

**Form 5754.** If the person receiving the winnings is not the actual winner or is a member of a group of winners, see the instructions for Form 5754, Statement by Person(s) Receiving Gambling Winnings, in the 2007 Instructions for Forms W-2G and 5754.

**Need help?** If you have questions about reporting on Form W-2G, call the information reporting customer service site toll free at 1-866-455-7438 or 304-263-8700 (not toll free). For TTY/TDD equipment, call 304-267-3367 (not toll free). The hours of operation are Monday through Friday from 8:30 a.m. to 4:30 p.m., Eastern time. The service site can also be reached by email at *mccirp@irs.gov.*

# Appendix A2
# Form 1099-MISC

*Miscellaneous Income* (Drawing or tournament win)

| ☐ VOID    ☐ CORRECTED | | |
|---|---|---|
| PAYER'S name, street address, city, state, ZIP code. and telephone no.<br><br>**Palms Hotel and Casino**<br>**4231 W Flamingo Road**<br>**Las Vegas, NV 89102** | **1** Rents<br>$<br>**2** Royalties<br>$<br>**3** Other income<br>$ 5,000 | OMB No. 1545-0115<br><br>20**07**<br>Form **1099-MISC**<br>**4** Federal income tax withheld<br>$ |
| | | **Miscellaneous Income** |
| PAYER'S federal identification number<br>**20-1234567** | RECIPIENT'S identification number<br>**123-45-6789** | **5** Fishing boat proceeds<br>$ | **6** Medical and health care payments<br>$ | **Copy 1**<br>**For State Tax Department** |

| RECIPIENT'S name<br><br>**Jean Scott** | **7** Nonemployee compensation<br>$ | **8** Substitute payments in lieu of dividends or interest<br>$ |
|---|---|---|
| Street address (including apt. no.)<br>**123 Main Street** | **9** Payer made direct sales of $5,000 or more of consumer products to a buyer (recipient) for resale ► ☐ | **10** Crop insurance proceeds<br>$ |
| City, state, and ZIP code<br>**Las Vegas NV 89102** | **11** | **12** |
| Account number (see instructions) | **13** Excess golden parachute payments<br>$ | **14** Gross proceeds paid to an attorney<br>$ |

| **15a** Section 409A deferrals<br>$ | **15b** Section 409A income<br>$ | **16** State tax withheld<br>$<br>$ | **17** State/Payer's state no. | **18** State income<br>$<br>$ |
|---|---|---|---|---|

Form **1099-MISC**       Department of the Treasury - Internal Revenue Service

## Appendix A2-continued
*Miscellaneous Income* (Instructions for Payers)

### Instructions for Payers

General and specific form instructions are provided as separate products. The products you should use to complete Form 1099-MISC are the 2007 General Instructions for Forms 1099, 1098, 5498, and W-2G and the 2007 Instructions for Form 1099-MISC. A chart in the general instructions gives a quick guide to which form must be filed to report a particular payment. To order these instructions and additional forms, visit the IRS website at www.irs.gov or call 1-800-TAX-FORM (1-800-829-3676).

**Caution:** *Because paper forms are scanned during processing, you cannot file with the IRS Forms 1096, 1098, 1099, or 5498 that you print from the IRS website.*

**Due dates.** Furnish Copy B of this form to the recipient by January 31, 2008.

File Copy A of this form with the IRS by February 28, 2008. If you file electronically, the due date is March 31, 2008. To file electronically, you must have software that generates a file according to the specifications in Pub. 1220, Specifications for Filing Forms 1098, 1099, 5498, and W-2G Electronically or Magnetically. IRS does not provide a fill-in form option.

**Need help?** If you have questions about reporting on Form 1099-MISC, call the information reporting customer service site toll free at 1-866-455-7438 or 304-263-8700 (not toll free). For TTY/TDD equipment, call 304-267-3367 (not toll free). The hours of operation are Monday through Friday from 8:30 a.m. to 4:30 p.m., Eastern time. The service site can also be reached by email at mccirp@irs.gov.

---

## *Miscellaneous Income* (Instructions for Recipients)

### Instructions for Recipients

**Account number.** May show an account or other unique number the payer assigned to distinguish your account.

**Amounts shown may be subject to self-employment (SE) tax.** If your net income from self-employment is $400 or more, you must file a return and compute your SE tax on Schedule SE (Form 1040). See Pub. 334, Tax Guide for Small Business, for more information. If no income or social security and Medicare taxes were withheld and you are still receiving these payments, see Form 1040-ES, Estimated Tax for Individuals. Individuals must report as explained for box 7 below. Corporations, fiduciaries, or partnerships report the amounts on the proper line of your tax return.

**Boxes 1 and 2.** Report rents from real estate on Schedule E (Form 1040). If you provided significant services to the tenant, sold real estate as a business, or rented personal property as a business, report on Schedule C or C-EZ (Form 1040). For royalties on timber, coal, and iron ore, see Pub. 544, Sales and Other Dispositions of Assets.

**Box 3.** Generally, report this amount on the "Other income" line of Form 1040 and identify the payment. The amount shown may be payments received as the beneficiary of a deceased employee, prizes, awards, taxable damages, Indian gaming profits, payments made by employers to former employees who are serving in the Armed Forces or the National Guard, or other taxable income. See Pub. 525, Taxable and Nontaxable Income. If it is trade or business income, report this amount on Schedule C, C-EZ, or F (Form 1040).

**Box 4.** Shows backup withholding or withholding on Indian gaming profits. Generally, a payer must backup withhold at a 28% rate if you did not furnish your taxpayer identification number. See Form W-9, Request for Taxpayer Identification Number and Certification, for more information. Report this amount on your income tax return as tax withheld.

**Box 5.** An amount in this box means the fishing boat operator considers you self-employed. Report this amount on Schedule C or C-EZ (Form 1040). See Pub. 334.

**Box 6.** For individuals, report on Schedule C or C-EZ (Form 1040).

**Box 7.** Shows nonemployee compensation. If you are in the trade or business of catching fish, box 7 may show cash you received for the sale of fish. If payments in this box are SE income, report this amount on Schedule C, C-EZ, or F (Form 1040), and complete Schedule SE (Form 1040). You received this form instead of Form W-2 because the payer did not consider you an employee and did not withhold income tax or social security and Medicare taxes. Contact the payer if you believe this form is incorrect or has been issued in error. If you believe you are an employee, call the IRS for information on how to report any social security and Medicare taxes or see Form 8919, Uncollected Social Security and Medicare Taxes on Wages.

**Box 8.** Shows substitute payments in lieu of dividends or tax-exempt interest received by your broker on your behalf as a result of a loan of your securities. Report on the "Other income" line of Form 1040.

**Box 9.** If checked, $5,000 or more of sales of consumer products was paid to you on a buy-sell, deposit-commission, or other basis. A dollar amount does not have to be shown. Generally, report any income from your sale of these products on Schedule C or C-EZ (Form 1040).

**Box 10.** Report this amount on line 8 of Schedule F (Form 1040).

**Box 13.** Shows your total compensation of excess golden parachute payments subject to a 20% excise tax. See the Form 1040 instructions for where to report.

**Box 14.** Shows gross proceeds paid to an attorney in connection with legal services. Report only the taxable part as income on your return.

**Box 15a.** Shows current year deferrals as a nonemployee under a nonqualified deferred compensation (NQDC) plan that is subject to the requirements of section 409A. Any earnings on current and prior year deferrals are also reported.

**Box 15b.** Shows income as a nonemployee under an NQDC plan that does not meet the requirements of section 409A. This amount is also included in box 7 as nonemployee compensation. Any amount included in box 15a that is currently taxable is also included in this box. This income is also subject to a substantial additional tax to be reported on Form 1040. See "Total Tax" in the Form 1040 instructions.

**Boxes 16-18.** Shows state or local income tax withheld from the payments.

## *Statement by Person(s) Receiving Gambling Winnings* (Group Win)

| Form **5754** (Rev. August 2005) Department of the Treasury Internal Revenue Service | **Statement by Person(s) Receiving Gambling Winnings** ► Recipients of gambling winnings should see the instructions on the back of this form. ► Payers of gambling winnings should see the separate Instructions for Forms W-2G and 5754. | | | OMB No. 1545-0239 Return to payer. Do not send to the IRS. |
|---|---|---|---|---|
| Date won **12/1/2006** | Type of winnings **SLOTS** | Game number | Machine number **X1432** | Race number |

### Part I    Person to Whom Winnings Are Paid

| Name | Address |
|---|---|
| Jean Scott | 123 Main Street Las Vegas NV 89102 |

| Taxpayer identification number | Other I.D. | Amount received | Federal income tax withheld |
|---|---|---|---|
| 123-45-6789 | | 500,000 | |

### Part II    Persons to Whom Winnings Are Taxable *(continued on page 2)*

| (a) Name | (b) Taxpayer identification number | (c) Address | (d) Amount won | (e) Winnings from identical wagers |
|---|---|---|---|---|
| Marissa Chien | 345-67-8912 | 234 Main Street Las Vegas NV 89102 | 250,000 | |
| Jean Scott | 123-45-6789 | 123 Main Street Las Vegas NV 89102 | 250,000 | |
| | | | | |
| | | | | |
| | | | | |
| | | | | |
| | | | | |
| | | | | |
| | | | | |

Under penalties of perjury, I declare that, to the best of my knowledge and belief, the names, addresses, and taxpayer identification numbers that I have furnished correctly identify me as the recipient of this payment and correctly identify each person entitled to any part of this payment and any payments from identical wagers.

Signature ►        Date ►

For Privacy Act and Paperwork Reduction Act Notice, see back of form.     Cat. No. 12100R     Form **5754** (Rev. 8-2005)

## Appendix A3-continued
# *Statement by Person(s) Receiving Gambling Winnings* (Group Win)

Form 5754 (Rev. 8-2005)                                                                                        Page **2**

| **Part II** | **Persons to Whom Winnings Are Taxable** *(continued from page 1)* | | | |
|---|---|---|---|---|
| (a) Name | (b) Taxpayer identification number | (c) Address | (d) Amount won | (e) Winnings from identical wagers |
| | | | | |
| | | | | |
| | | | | |
| | | | | |

### Instructions for Recipient of Gambling Winnings

**Purpose of form.** You must complete Form 5754 if you receive gambling winnings either for someone else or as a member of a group of winners on the same winning ticket. The information you provide on the form enables the payer of the winnings to prepare Form W-2G, Certain Gambling Winnings, for each winner to show the winnings taxable to each.

**Completing the form.** If you are the person to whom gambling winnings are paid, enter your name, address, and taxpayer identification number in Part I. If the winnings are from state-conducted lotteries, the box labeled "Other I.D." may be left blank. The total amount received and the total federal income tax withheld must be entered in the remaining columns.

Complete Part II to identify each winner and each winner's share of the winnings. If you are also one of the winners, enter your information first in Part II by entering "Same as above" in columns (a), (b), and (c) and the applicable amounts in columns (d) and (e). Then complete columns (a) through (e) for each of the other winners. Return the form to the payer.

**Taxpayer identification number.** The taxpayer identification number for an individual is the social security number or individual taxpayer identification number. For all others, it is the employer identification number.

**Signature.** If federal income tax is withheld, the person who receives the winnings must sign and date the form. If no federal income tax is withheld, no signature is required.

**Privacy Act and Paperwork Reduction Act Notice.** We ask for the information on this form to carry out the Internal Revenue laws of the United States. You are required to give us the information. We need it to ensure that you are complying with these laws and to allow us to figure and collect the right amount of tax. Regulations section 31.3402(q) requires you to furnish an information return to the payer if you receive gambling winnings either for someone else or as a member of a group of winners on the same winning ticket. Section 6109 and its regulations require you to show your taxpayer identification number to persons who must file information returns with the IRS to report certain information. Routine uses of this information include giving it to the Department of Justice for civil and criminal litigation, and to cities, states, and the District of Columbia for use in administering their tax laws. We may also disclose this information to other countries under a tax treaty, to federal and state agencies to enforce federal nontax criminal laws, or to federal law enforcement and intelligence agencies to combat terrorism. If you fail to provide this information in a timely manner, you may be subject to penalties.

You are not required to provide the information requested on a form that is subject to the Paperwork Reduction Act unless the form displays a valid OMB control number. Books or records relating to a form or its instructions must be retained as long as their contents may become material in the administration of any Internal Revenue law. Generally, tax returns and return information are confidential, as required by section 6103.

The time needed to complete this form will vary depending on individual circumstances. The estimated average time is 12 minutes.

If you have comments concerning the accuracy of this time estimate or suggestions for making this form simpler, we would be happy to hear from you. You can write to the Internal Revenue Service, Tax Products Coordinating Committee, SE:W:CAR:MP:T:T:SP, 1111 Constitution Avenue, NW, IR-6406, Washington, DC 20224. Do not send this form to this address. Instead, return it to the payer.

Form **5754** (Rev. 8-2005)

*Application for IRS Individual Taxpayer ID Number*

| Form **W-7** (Rev. January 2007) Department of the Treasury Internal Revenue Service | **Application for IRS Individual Taxpayer Identification Number** ► See instructions. ► For use by individuals who are not U.S. citizens or permanent residents. | OMB No. 1545-0074 |
|---|---|---|

An IRS individual taxpayer identification number (ITIN) is for federal tax purposes only.

**FOR IRS USE ONLY**

**Before you begin:**
- **Do not submit** this form if you have, or are eligible to obtain, a U.S. social security number (SSN).
- Getting an ITIN does not change your immigration status or your right to work in the United States and does not make you eligible for the earned income credit.

**Reason you are submitting Form W-7.** Read the instructions for the box you check. **Caution:** If you check box **b**, **c**, **d**, **e**, **f**, or **g**, you must file a tax return with Form W-7 unless you meet one of the exceptions (see instructions).

- a ☐ Nonresident alien required to obtain ITIN to claim tax treaty benefit
- b ☐ Nonresident alien filing a U.S. tax return
- c ☐ U.S. resident alien **(based on days present in the United States)** filing a U.S. tax return
- d ☐ Dependent of U.S. citizen/resident alien ⎤ Enter name and SSN/ITIN of U.S. citizen/resident alien (see instructions) ► ...............
- e ☐ Spouse of U.S. citizen/resident alien ⎦
- f ☐ Nonresident alien student, professor, or researcher filing a U.S. tax return or claiming an exception
- g ☐ Dependent/spouse of a nonresident alien holding a U.S. visa
- h ☐ Other (see instructions) ► ...................................................................................

Additional information for **a** and **f**: Enter treaty country ► .................... and treaty article number ► ..............

| **Name** (see instructions) | **1a** First name | Middle name | Last name |
|---|---|---|---|
| Name at birth if different . . . ► | **1b** First name | Middle name | Last name |

| **Applicant's mailing address** | **2** Street address, apartment number, or rural route number. **If you have a P.O. box, see page 4.** |
|---|---|
| | City or town, state or province, and country. Include ZIP code or postal code where appropriate. |

| **Foreign address** (if different from above) (see instructions) | **3** Street address, apartment number, or rural route number. **Do not use a P.O. box number.** |
|---|---|
| | City or town, state or province, and country. Include ZIP code or postal code where appropriate. |

| **Birth information** | **4** Date of birth (month / day / year) / / | Country of birth | City and state or province (optional) | **5** ☐ Male ☐ Female |
|---|---|---|---|---|

| **Other information** | **6a** Country(ies) of citizenship | **6b** Foreign tax I.D. number (if any) | **6c** Type of U.S. visa (if any), number, and expiration date |
|---|---|---|---|

**6d** Identification document(s) submitted (see instructions)
☐ Passport   ☐ Driver's license/State I.D.   ☐ USCIS documentation   ☐ Other ...................
Issued by: ..........   No.: ..........   Exp. date: / /   Entry date in U.S. / /

**6e** Have you previously received a U.S. temporary taxpayer identification number (TIN) or employer identification number (EIN)?
☐ **No/Do not know.** Skip line 6f.
☐ **Yes.** Complete line 6f. If more than one, list on a sheet and attach to this form (see instructions).

**6f** Enter: TIN or EIN ► .................................................................. and
Name under which it was issued ►

**6g** Name of college/university or company (see instructions) ......................
City and state ..........   Length of stay ..........

| **Sign Here** | Under penalties of perjury, I (applicant/delegate/acceptance agent) declare that I have examined this application, including accompanying documentation and statements, and to the best of my knowledge and belief, it is true, correct, and complete. I authorize the IRS to disclose to my acceptance agent or return information necessary to resolve matters regarding the assignment of my IRS individual taxpayer identification number (ITIN), including any previously assigned taxpayer identifying number. |
|---|---|

| | Signature of applicant (if delegate, see instructions) ► | Date (month / day / year) / / | Phone number ( ) |
|---|---|---|---|
| Keep a copy for your records. | Name of delegate, if applicable (type or print) | Delegate's relationship to applicant ► | ☐ Parent ☐ Court-appointed guardian ☐ Power of Attorney |

| **Acceptance Agent's Use ONLY** | Signature | Date (month / day / year) / / | Phone ( ) |
|---|---|---|---|
| | | | Fax ( ) |
| | Name and title (type or print) | Name of company | EIN |
| | | | EFIN/Office Code |

For Paperwork Reduction Act Notice, see page 4.   Cat. No. 10229L   Form **W-7** (Rev. 1-2007)

*Foreign Person's U.S. Source Income Subject to Withholding*

| Form **1042-S** | Foreign Person's U.S. Source Income Subject to Withholding | 2007 | OMB No. 1545-0096 |
|---|---|---|---|
| Department of the Treasury Internal Revenue Service | ☐ AMENDED | ☐ PRO-RATA BASIS REPORTING | **Copy A** for Internal Revenue Service |

| 1 Income code | 2 Gross income | 3 Withholding allowances | 4 Net income | 5 Tax rate | 6 Exemption code | 7 U.S. Federal tax withheld | 8 Amount repaid to recipient |
|---|---|---|---|---|---|---|---|
| | | | | | | | |

**9** Withholding agent's EIN ▶ ☐ EIN ☐ QI-EIN

**14** Recipient's U.S. TIN, if any ▶ ☐ SSN or ITIN ☐ EIN ☐ QI-EIN

**10a** WITHHOLDING AGENT'S name

**15** Recipient's country of residence for tax purposes | **16** Country code

**10b** Address (number and street)

**17** NONQUALIFIED INTERMEDIARY'S (NQI's)/ FLOW-THROUGH ENTITY'S name | **18** Country code

**10c** Additional address line (room or suite no.)

**10d** City or town, province or state, and country | **10e** ZIP code or foreign postal code

**19a** NQI's/Flow-through entity's address (number and street)

**19b** Additional address line (room or suite no.)

**11** Recipient's account number (optional) | **12** Recipient code

**19c** City or town, province or state, and country | **19d** ZIP code or foreign postal code

**13a** RECIPIENT'S name

**20** NQI's/Flow-through entity's TIN, if any ▶

**13b** Address (number and street)

**21** PAYER'S name and TIN (if different from withholding agent's)

**13c** Additional address line (room or suite no.)

**13d** City or town, province or state, and country | **13e** ZIP code or foreign postal code | **22** State income tax withheld | **23** Payer's state tax no. | **24** Name of state

For Privacy Act and Paperwork Reduction Act Notice, see page 16 of the separate instructions.    Cat. No. 11386R    Form **1042-S** (2007)

# Appendix A5-continued
## *U.S. Income Tax Filing Requirements*

**U.S. Income Tax Filing Requirements**

Generally, every nonresident alien individual, nonresident alien fiduciary, and foreign corporation with United States income, including income that is effectively connected with the conduct of a trade or business in the United States, must file a United States income tax return. However, no return is required to be filed by a nonresident alien individual, nonresident alien fiduciary, or a foreign corporation if such person was not engaged in a trade or business in the United States at any time during the tax year and if the tax liability of such person was fully satisfied by the withholding of United States tax at the source. (Corporations file Form 1120-F; all others file Form 1040NR (or Form 1040NR-EZ if eligible).) You may get the return forms and instructions at any United States Embassy or consulate or by writing to: National Distribution Center, P.O. Box 8903, Bloomington, IL 61702-8903, U.S.A.

En règle générale, tout étranger non-résident, tout organisme fidéicommissaire étranger non-résident et toute société étrangère percevant un revenu aux Etats-Unis, y compris tout revenu dérivé, en fait, du fonctionnement d'un commerce ou d'une affaire aux Etats-Unis, doit soumettre aux Etats-Unis, une déclaration d'impôt sur le revenu. Cependant aucune déclaration d'impôt sur le revenu n'est exigée d'un étranger non-résident, d'un organisme fidéicommissaire étrange non-résident, ou d'une société étrangère s'ils n'ont pris part à aucun commerce ou affaire aux Etats-Unis à aucun moment pendant l'année fiscale et si les impôts dont ils sont redevables, ont été entièrement acquittés par une retenue à la source, de leur montant. (Les sociétés doivent faire leur déclaration d'impôt en remplissant le formulaire 1120-F; tous les autres redevables doivent remplir le formulaire 1040NR (ou 1040NR-EZ si éligible).) On peut se procurer formulaires de déclarations d'impôts et instructions dans toutes les Ambassades et les Consulats des Etats-Unis. L'on peut également s'adresser pour tous renseignements a: National Distribution Center, P.O. Box 8903, Bloomington, IL 61702-8903, U.S.A.

Por regla general, todo extranjero no residente, todo organismo fideicomisario extranjero no residente y toda sociedad anónima extranjera que reciba ingresos en los Estados Unidos, incluyendo ingresos relacionados con la conducción de un negocio o comercio dentro de los Estados Unidos, deberá presentar una declaración estadounidense de impuestos sobre ingreso. Sin embargo, no se requiere declaración alguna a un individuo extranjero no residente, una sociedad anónima extranjera u organismo fideicomisario extranjero no residente, si tal persona no ha efectuado comercio o negocio en los Estados Unidos durante el año fiscal y si la responsabilidad con los impuestos de tal persona ha sido satisfecha plenamente mediante retención del impuesto de los Estados Unidos en la fuente. (Las sociedades anónimas envían la Forma 1120-F; todos los demás contribuyentes envían la Forma 1040NR (o la Forma 1040NR-EZ si le corresponde).) Se podrán obtener formas e instrucciones en cualquier Embajada o Consulado de los Estados Unidos o escribiendo directamente a: National Distribution Center, P.O. Box 8903, Bloomington, IL 61702-8903, U.S.A.

Im allgemeinen muss jede ausländische Einzelperson, jeder ausländische Bevollmächtigte und jede ausländische Gesellschaft mit Einkommen in den Vereinigten Staaten, einschliesslich des Einkommens, welches direkt mit der Ausübung von Handel oder Gewerbe innerhalb der Staaten verbunden ist, eine Einkommensteuererklärung der Vereinigten Staaten abgeben. Eine Erklärung, muss jedoch nicht von Ausländern, ausländischen Bevollmächtigten oder ausländischen Gesellschaften in den Vereinigten Staaten eingereicht werden, falls eine solche Person während des Steuerjahres kein Gewerbe oder Handel in den Vereinigten Staaten ausgeübt hat und die Steuerschuld durch Einbehaltung der Steuern der Vereinigten Staaten durch die Einkommensquelle abgegolten ist. (Gesellschaften reichen den Vordruck 1120-F ein; alle anderen reichen das Formblatt 1040NR oder wenn passend das Formblatt 1040NR-EZ ein.) Einkommensteuererklärungen und Instruktionen können bei den Botschaften und Konsulaten der Vereinigten Staaten eingeholt werden. Um weitere Informationen wende man sich bitte an: National Distribution Center, P.O. Box 8903, Bloomington, IL 61702-8903, U.S.A.

---

# *U.S. Income Tax Filing Explanation of Codes*

**Explanation of Codes**

Box 1. Income code.

| Code | Types of Income |
|---|---|
| 01 | Interest paid by U.S. obligors—general |
| 02 | Interest paid on real property mortgages |
| 03 | Interest paid to controlling foreign corporations |
| 04 | Interest paid by foreign corporations |
| 05 | Interest on tax-free covenant bonds |
| 29 | Deposit interest |
| 30 | Original issue discount (OID) |
| 31 | Short-term OID |
| 33 | Substitute payment—interest |
| 06 | Dividends paid by U.S. corporations—general |
| 07 | Dividends qualifying for direct dividend rate |
| 08 | Dividends paid by foreign corporations |
| 34 | Substitute payment—dividends |
| 09 | Capital gains |
| 10 | Industrial royalties |
| 11 | Motion picture or television copyright royalties |
| 12 | Other royalties (for example, copyright, recording, publishing) |
| 13 | Real property income and natural resources royalties |
| 14 | Pensions, annuities, alimony, and/or insurance premiums |
| 15 | Scholarship or fellowship grants |
| 16 | Compensation for independent personal services[1] |
| 17 | Compensation for dependent personal services[1] |
| 18 | Compensation for teaching[1] |
| 19 | Compensation during studying and training[1] |
| 20 | Earnings as an artist or athlete[1] |
| 24 | Real estate investment trust (REIT) distributions of capital gains |
| 25 | Trust distributions subject to IRC section 1445 |
| 26 | Unsevered growing crops and timber distributions by a trust subject to IRC section 1445 |
| 27 | Publicly traded partnership distributions subject to IRC section 1446 |
| 28 | Gambling winnings[6] |
| 32 | Notional principal contract income[3] |
| 35 | Substitute payment—other |
| 36 | Capital gains distributions |
| 37 | Return of capital |
| 50 | Other income |

Box 6. Exemption code (applies if the tax rate entered in box 5 is 00.00).

| Code | Authority for Exemption |
|---|---|
| 01 | Income effectively connected with a U.S. trade or business |
| 02 | Exempt under an Internal Revenue Code section (income other than portfolio interest) |
| 03 | Income is not from U.S. sources[4] |
| 04 | Exempt under tax treaty |
| 05 | Portfolio interest exempt under an Internal Revenue Code section |
| 06 | Qualified intermediary that assumes primary withholding responsibility |
| 07 | Withholding foreign partnership or withholding foreign trust |
| 08 | U.S. branch treated as a U.S. person |
| 09 | Qualified intermediary represents income is exempt |

Box 12. Recipient code.

| Code | Type of Recipient |
|---|---|
| 01 | Individual[2] |
| 02 | Corporation[2] |
| 03 | Partnership other than withholding foreign partnership[2] |
| 04 | Withholding foreign partnership or withholding foreign trust |
| 05 | Trust |
| 06 | Government or international organization |
| 07 | Tax-exempt organization (IRC section 501(a)) |
| 08 | Private foundation |
| 09 | Artist or athlete[2] |
| 10 | Estate |
| 11 | U.S. branch treated as U.S. person |
| 12 | Qualified intermediary |
| 13 | Private arrangement intermediary withholding rate pool—general[5] |
| 14 | Private arrangement intermediary withholding rate pool—exempt organizations[5] |
| 15 | Qualified intermediary withholding rate pool—general[5] |
| 16 | Qualified intermediary withholding rate pool—exempt organizations[5] |
| 17 | Authorized foreign agent |
| 18 | Public pension fund |
| 20 | Unknown recipient |

---

[1] If compensation that otherwise would be covered under Income Codes 16–19 is directly attributable to the recipient's occupation as an artist or athlete, use Income Code 20 instead
[2] If Income Code 20 is used, Recipient Code 09 (artist or athlete) should be used instead of Recipient Code 01 (individual), 02 (corporation), or 03 (partnership other than withholding foreign partnership).
[3] Use appropriate Interest Income Code for embedded interest in a notional principal contract.
[4] Non-U.S. source income received by a nonresident alien is not subject to U.S. tax. Use Exemption Code 03 when entering an amount for information reporting purposes only.
[5] May be used only by a qualified intermediary.
[6] Subject to 30% withholding rate unless the recipient is from one of the treaty countries listed under Gambling winnings (Income Code 28) in Pub. 515.

# Sample Tax Forms

## Appendix B1
## Recreational Gambler—Non-Itemized

### Form 1040 *side 1*

| | | | | | |
|---|---|---|---|---|---|
| Form **1040** | Department of the Treasury — Internal Revenue Service **U.S. Individual Income Tax Return** | **2006** | (99) | IRS Use Only — Do not write or staple in this space. | |

For the year Jan 1 - Dec 31, 2006, or other tax year beginning , 2006, ending , 20    OMB No. 1545-0074

**Label** (See instructions.)
**Use the IRS label.** Otherwise, please print or type.

Your first name: JEAN  MI  Last name: SCOTT  —  Your social security number: 123-45-6789

If a joint return, spouse's first name: BRAD  MI  Last name: SCOTT  —  Spouse's social security number: 234-56-7891

Home address (number and street). If you have a P.O. box, see instructions.: 123 MAIN STREET  Apartment no.

City, town or post office. If you have a foreign address, see instructions.: LAS VEGAS  State: NV  ZIP code: 89102

► You **must** enter your social security number(s) above. ◄

Checking a box below will not change your tax or refund.

**Presidential Election Campaign** ► Check here if you, or your spouse if filing jointly, want $3 to go to this fund? (see instructions) ........ ► ☐ You ☐ Spouse

**Filing Status**
Check only one box.
1 ☐ Single
2 ☒ Married filing jointly (even if only one had income)
3 ☐ Married filing separately. Enter spouse's SSN above & full name here ►
4 ☐ Head of household (with qualifying person). (See instructions.) If the qualifying person is a child but not your dependent, enter this child's name here ►
5 ☐ Qualifying widow(er) with dependent child (see instructions)

**Exemptions**
6a ☒ **Yourself.** If someone can claim you as a dependent, **do not** check box 6a ...........
b ☒ **Spouse** ...........

Boxes checked on 6a and 6b: **2**

c **Dependents:**
| (1) First name   Last name | (2) Dependent's social security number | (3) Dependent's relationship to you | (4) ✓ if qualifying child for child tax credit (see instrs) |
|---|---|---|---|
| | | | ☐ |
| | | | ☐ |
| | | | ☐ |
| | | | ☐ |

No. of children on 6c who: ● lived with you ... ● did not live with you due to divorce or separation (see instrs)

Dependents on 6c not entered above

If more than four dependents, see instructions.

d Total number of exemptions claimed ...........  Add numbers on lines above ► **2**

**Income**

Attach Form(s) W-2 here. Also attach Forms W-2G and 1099-R if tax was withheld.

If you did not get a W-2, see instructions.

Enclose, but do not attach, any payment. Also, please use Form 1040-V.

| | | |
|---|---|---|
| 7 Wages, salaries, tips, etc. Attach Form(s) W-2 ........... | **7** | 25,000. |
| 8a Taxable interest. Attach Schedule B if required ........... | **8a** | 1,000. |
| b Tax-exempt interest. Do not include on line 8a ... | 8b | |
| 9a Ordinary dividends. Attach Schedule B if required ........... | **9a** | |
| b Qualified dividends (see instrs) ... | 9b | |
| 10 Taxable refunds, credits, or offsets of state and local income taxes (see instructions) ... | **10** | |
| 11 Alimony received ... | **11** | |
| 12 Business income or (loss). Attach Schedule C or C-EZ... | **12** | |
| 13 Capital gain or (loss). Att Sch D if reqd. If not reqd, ck here ► ☐ | **13** | |
| 14 Other gains or (losses). Attach Form 4797 ... | **14** | |
| 15a IRA distributions ... 15a | b Taxable amount (see instrs) | **15b** | |
| 16a Pensions and annuities ... 16a | b Taxable amount (see instrs) | **16b** | |
| 17 Rental real estate, royalties, partnerships, S corporations, trusts, etc. Attach Schedule E | **17** | |
| 18 Farm income or (loss). Attach Schedule F ... | **18** | |
| 19 Unemployment compensation ... | **19** | |
| 20a Social security benefits ... 20a | b Taxable amount (see instrs) | **20b** | |
| 21 Other income GAMBLING WINNINGS | **21** | 5,000. ❶ |
| 22 Add the amounts in the far right column for lines 7 through 21. This is your **total income** ► | **22** | 31,000. |

**Adjusted Gross Income**

| | | |
|---|---|---|
| 23 Archer MSA deduction. Attach Form 8853 ... | 23 | |
| 24 Certain business expenses of reservists, performing artists, and fee-basis government officials. Attach Form 2106 or 2106-EZ ... | 24 | |
| 25 Health savings account deduction. Attach Form 8889 ... | 25 | |
| 26 Moving expenses. Attach Form 3903 ... | 26 | |
| 27 One-half of self-employment tax. Attach Schedule SE ... | 27 | |
| 28 Self-employed SEP, SIMPLE, and qualified plans ... | 28 | |
| 29 Self-employed health insurance deduction (see instructions) ... | 29 | |
| 30 Penalty on early withdrawal of savings ... | 30 | |
| 31a Alimony paid b Recipient's SSN ... ► | 31a | |
| 32 IRA deduction (see instructions) ... | 32 | |
| 33 Student loan interest deduction (see instructions) ... | 33 | |
| 34 Jury duty pay you gave to your employer ... | 34 | |
| 35 Domestic production activities deduction. Attach Form 8903 ... | 35 | |
| 36 Add lines 23 - 31a and 32 - 35 ... | 36 | |
| 37 Subtract line 36 from line 22. This is your **adjusted gross income** ... ► | 37 | 31,000. |

**BAA For Disclosure, Privacy Act, and Paperwork Reduction Act Notice, see instructions.**   FDIA0112  11/07/06   Form **1040** (2006)

Gambling gross win total for the year was $5,000❶. Gambling gross loss total was $6,000. The standard deduction is $10,300. Since gambling losses have

## Appendix B1-continued
# Form 1040 *side 2*

| Form **1040** (2006) | JEAN & BRAD SCOTT | 123-45-6789 | Page **2** |
|---|---|---|---|

| | | | |
|---|---|---|---|
| **Tax and Credits** | 38 Amount from line 37 (adjusted gross income) | 38 | 31,000. |
| **Standard Deduction for –** | 39a Check if: ☐ You were born before January 2, 1942, ☐ Blind. **Total boxes** ☐ Spouse was born before January 2, 1942, ☐ Blind. **checked** ► 39a ☐ | | |
| • People who checked any box on line 39a or 39b or who can be claimed as a dependent, see instructions. | b If your spouse itemizes on a separate return, or you were a dual-status alien, see instrs and ck here ► 39b ☐ | | |
| | 40 Itemized deductions (from Schedule A) or your **standard deduction** (see left margin) | 40 | 10,300. ❷ |
| | 41 Subtract line 40 from line 38 | 41 | 20,700. |
| • All others: | 42 If line 38 is over $112,875, or you provided housing to a person displaced by Hurricane Katrina, see instructions. Otherwise, multiply $3,300 by the total number of exemptions claimed on line 6d | 42 | 6,600. |
| Single or Married filing separately, $5,150 | 43 **Taxable income.** Subtract line 42 from line 41. If line 42 is more than line 41, enter -0- | 43 | 14,100. |
| Married filing jointly or Qualifying widow(er), $10,300 | 44 Tax (see instrs). Check if any tax is from: **a** ☐ Form(s) 8814 **b** ☐ Form 4972 | 44 | 1,413. |
| | 45 **Alternative minimum tax** (see instructions). Attach Form 6251 | 45 | |
| Head of household, $7,550 | 46 Add lines 44 and 45 | ► 46 | 1,413. |
| | 47 Foreign tax credit. Attach Form 1116 if required ... 47 | | |
| | 48 Credit for child and dependent care expenses. Attach Form 2441 ... 48 | | |
| | 49 Credit for the elderly or the disabled. Attach Schedule R .. 49 | | |
| | 50 Education credits. Attach Form 8863 ... 50 | | |
| | 51 Retirement savings contributions credit. Attach Form 8880 ... 51 | | |
| | 52 Residential energy credits. Attach Form 5695 ... 52 | | |
| | 53 Child tax credit (see instructions). Attach Form 8901 if required ... 53 | | |
| | 54 Credits from: **a** ☐ Form 8396 **b** ☐ Form 8839 **c** ☐ Form 8859 ... 54 | | |
| | 55 Other credits. Check applicable box(es): **a** ☐ Form 3800 **b** ☐ Form 8801 **c** ☐ Form _____ ... 55 | | |
| | 56 Add lines 47 through 55. These are your **total credits** | 56 | |
| | 57 Subtract line 56 from line 46. If line 56 is more than line 46, enter -0- | ► 57 | 1,413. |
| **Other Taxes** | 58 Self-employment tax. Attach Schedule SE | 58 | |
| | 59 Social security and Medicare tax on tip income not reported to employer. Attach Form 4137 | 59 | |
| | 60 Additional tax on IRAs, other qualified retirement plans, etc. Attach Form 5329 if required | 60 | |
| | 61 Advance earned income credit payments from Form(s) W-2, box 9 | 61 | |
| | 62 Household employment taxes. Attach Schedule H | 62 | |
| | 63 Add lines 57-62. This is your **total tax** | ► 63 | 1,413. |
| **Payments** | 64 Federal income tax withheld from Forms W-2 and 1099 ... 64 | 800. | |
| If you have a qualifying child, attach Schedule EIC. | 65 2006 estimated tax payments and amount applied from 2005 return ... 65 | | |
| | 66a Earned income credit (EIC) ... 66a | | |
| | b Nontaxable combat pay election ... 66b | | |
| | 67 Excess social security and tier 1 RRTA tax withheld (see instructions) ... 67 | | |
| | 68 Additional child tax credit. Attach Form 8812 ... 68 | | |
| | 69 Amount paid with request for extension to file (see instructions) ... 69 | | |
| | 70 Payments from: **a** ☐ Form 2439 **c** ☐ Form 8885 ... 70 | | |
| | 71 Credit for federal telephone excise tax paid. Attach Form 8913 if required ... 71 | 40. | |
| | 72 Add lines 64, 65, 66a, and 67 through 71. These are your **total payments** | ► 72 | 840. |
| **Refund** | 73 If line 72 is more than line 63, subtract line 63 from line 72. This is the amount you **overpaid** | 73 | |
| Direct deposit? See instructions and fill in 74b, 74c, and 74d or Form 8888. | 74a Amount of line 73 you want **refunded to you.** If Form 8888 is attached, check here ► ☐ | 74a | |
| | ► b Routing number ____ ► c Type: ☐ Checking ☐ Savings | | |
| | ► d Account number ____ | | |
| | 75 Amount of line 73 you want applied to your 2007 estimated tax ... ► 75 | | |
| **Amount You Owe** | 76 **Amount you owe.** Subtract line 72 from line 63. For details on how to pay, see instructions | ► 76 | 573. |
| | 77 Estimated tax penalty (see instructions) ... 77 | | |
| **Third Party Designee** | Do you want to allow another person to discuss this return with the IRS (see instructions)? ☐ **Yes.** Complete the following. ☒ **No** Designee's name ► _____ Phone no. ► _____ Personal identification number (PIN) ► _____ | | |
| **Sign Here** Joint return? See instructions. Keep a copy for your records. | Under penalties of perjury, I declare that I have examined this return and accompanying schedules and statements, and to the best of my knowledge and belief, they are true, correct, and complete. Declaration of preparer (other than taxpayer) is based on all information of which preparer has any knowledge. | | |
| | Your signature ► | Date | Your occupation REC GAMBLER | Daytime phone number |
| | Spouse's signature. If a joint return, **both** must sign. ► | Date | Spouse's occupation REC GAMBLER | |
| **Paid Preparer's Use Only** | Preparer's signature ► Shin-Chi Chien, EA | Date 08/07/2007 | Check if self-employed ☐ | Preparer's SSN or PTIN P00039748 |
| | Firm's name (or yours if self-employed), address, and ZIP code ► ADVANTAGE TAX PLUS 2649 W. HORIZON RIDGE PKWY #120 HENDERSON NV 89052 | | EIN 30-0003336 | Phone no. (702) 207-1040 |

Form **1040** (2006)

to be claimed as an itemized deduction and taxpayers have only a few small other deductions, it is better to take the standard deduction❷ than to itemize. This results in paying tax on *gross* wins even though taxpayers have an actual net gambling loss of $1,000 for the year.

# Appendix B2
# Recreational Gambler—Itemized

## Form 1040 *side 1*

| Form **1040** | Department of the Treasury — Internal Revenue Service **U.S. Individual Income Tax Return** | **2006** | (99) | IRS Use Only — Do not write or staple in this space. |
|---|---|---|---|---|

For the year Jan 1 - Dec 31, 2006, or other tax year beginning , 2006, ending , 20 — OMB No. 1545-0074

**Label** (See instructions.)

| | Your first name | MI | Last name | Your social security number |
|---|---|---|---|---|
| | JEAN | | SCOTT | 123-45-6789 |
| | If a joint return, spouse's first name | MI | Last name | Spouse's social security number |
| | BRAD | | SCOTT | 234-56-7891 |

**Use the IRS label. Otherwise, please print or type.**

Home address (number and street). If you have a P.O. box, see instructions. — Apartment no.
123 MAIN STREET

You **must** enter your social security number(s) above. ▲

City, town or post office. If you have a foreign address, see instructions. — State — ZIP code
LAS VEGAS — NV — 89102

Checking a box below will not change your tax or refund.

**Presidential Election Campaign** ▶ Check here if you, or your spouse if filing jointly, want $3 to go to this fund? (see instructions) .......... ▶ ☐ You ☐ Spouse

**Filing Status**
Check only one box.

1 ☐ Single
2 ☒ Married filing jointly (even if only one had income)
3 ☐ Married filing separately. Enter spouse's SSN above & full name here ▶
4 ☐ Head of household (with qualifying person). (See instructions.) If the qualifying person is a child but not your dependent, enter this child's name here ▶
5 ☐ Qualifying widow(er) with dependent child (see instructions)

**Exemptions**

6a ☒ Yourself. If someone can claim you as a dependent, **do not** check box 6a ..........
b ☒ Spouse ..................................................

Boxes checked on 6a and 6b  **2**

c Dependents:

| (1) First name   Last name | (2) Dependent's social security number | (3) Dependent's relationship to you | (4) ✓ if qualifying child for child tax credit (see instrs) |
|---|---|---|---|

No. of children on 6c who:
• lived with you
• did not live with you due to divorce or separation (see instrs)

If more than four dependents, see instructions.

Dependents on 6c not entered above

d Total number of exemptions claimed .................................... ▶

Add numbers on lines above ▶ **2**

**Income**

Attach Form(s) W-2 here. Also attach Forms W-2G and 1099-R if tax was withheld.

If you did not get a W-2, see instructions.

Enclose, but do not attach, any payment. Also, please use Form 1040-V.

| 7 Wages, salaries, tips, etc. Attach Form(s) W-2 ...................... | 7 | 25,000. |
|---|---|---|
| 8a Taxable interest. Attach Schedule B if required ..................... | 8a | 1,000. |
| b Tax-exempt interest. **Do not** include on line 8a ....... 8b | | |
| 9a Ordinary dividends. Attach Schedule B if required .................. | 9a | |
| b Qualified dividends (see instrs) .................... 9b | | |
| 10 Taxable refunds, credits, or offsets of state and local income taxes (see instructions) .... | 10 | |
| 11 Alimony received .................................................. | 11 | |
| 12 Business income or (loss). Attach Schedule C or C-EZ ............... | 12 | |
| 13 Capital gain or (loss). Att Sch D if reqd. If not reqd, ck here ............. ▶ ☐ | 13 | |
| 14 Other gains or (losses). Attach Form 4797 ......................... | 14 | |
| 15a IRA distributions ......... 15a | b Taxable amount (see instrs) .. 15b | |
| 16a Pensions and annuities .... 16a | b Taxable amount (see instrs) .. 16b | |
| 17 Rental real estate, royalties, partnerships, S corporations, trusts, etc. Attach Schedule E .. | 17 | |
| 18 Farm income or (loss). Attach Schedule F ........................... | 18 | |
| 19 Unemployment compensation ...................................... | 19 | |
| 20a Social security benefits ... 20a | b Taxable amount (see instrs) .. 20b | |
| 21 Other income GAMBLING WINNINGS .............................. | 21 | 50,000. ❸ |
| 22 Add the amounts in the far right column for lines 7 through 21. This is your **total income** ▶ | 22 | 76,000. |

**Adjusted Gross Income**

| 23 Archer MSA deduction. Attach Form 8853 ........ | 23 | | |
|---|---|---|---|
| 24 Certain business expenses of reservists, performing artists, and fee-basis government officials. Attach Form 2106 or 2106-EZ ...... | 24 | | |
| 25 Health savings account deduction. Attach Form 8889 ....... | 25 | | |
| 26 Moving expenses. Attach Form 3903 ................. | 26 | | |
| 27 One-half of self-employment tax. Attach Schedule SE .... | 27 | | |
| 28 Self-employed SEP, SIMPLE, and qualified plans ...... | 28 | | |
| 29 Self-employed health insurance deduction (see instructions) ........... | 29 | | |
| 30 Penalty on early withdrawal of savings .................. | 30 | | |
| 31a Alimony paid b Recipient's SSN .... ▶ | 31a | | |
| 32 IRA deduction (see instructions) ...................... | 32 | | |
| 33 Student loan interest deduction (see instructions) .......... | 33 | | |
| 34 Jury duty pay you gave to your employer ................ | 34 | | |
| 35 Domestic production activities deduction. Attach Form 8903 ......... | 35 | | |
| 36 Add lines 23 - 31a and 32 - 35 ................................... | | 36 | |
| 37 Subtract line 36 from line 22. This is your **adjusted gross income** ............. ▶ | | 37 | 76,000. |

BAA For Disclosure, Privacy Act, and Paperwork Reduction Act Notice, see instructions. — FDIA0112 11/07/06 — Form **1040** (2006)

In this scenario, the taxpayers are not "penalized" for gambling. Their other itemized deductions, such as mortgage interest and real estate taxes, already put them over the standard deduction amount for a married couple. Therefore, the

## Appendix B2-continued
# Form 1040 *side 2*

| Form 1040 (2006) | JEAN & BRAD SCOTT | | 123-45-6789 | Page 2 |
|---|---|---|---|---|

| Tax and Credits | 38 | Amount from line 37 (adjusted gross income) | 38 | 76,000. |
|---|---|---|---|---|
| **Standard Deduction for –** • People who checked any box on line 39a or 39b or who can be claimed as a dependent, see instructions. • All others: Single or Married filing separately, $5,150 Married filing jointly or Qualifying widow(er), $10,300 Head of household, $7,550 | 39a | Check if: ☐ You were born before January 2, 1942, ☐ Blind. ☐ Spouse was born before January 2, 1942, ☐ Blind. Total boxes checked ► 39a | | |
| | b | If your spouse itemizes on a separate return, or you were a dual-status alien, see instrs and ck here ► 39b ☐ | | |
| | 40 | Itemized deductions (from Schedule A) or your standard deduction (see left margin) | 40 | 63,999. |
| | 41 | Subtract line 40 from line 38 | 41 | 12,001. |
| | 42 | If line 38 is over $112,875, or you provided housing to a person displaced by Hurricane Katrina, see instructions. Otherwise, multiply $3,300 by the total number of exemptions claimed on line 6d | 42 | 6,600. |
| | 43 | Taxable income. Subtract line 42 from line 41. If line 42 is more than line 41, enter -0- | 43 | 5,401. |
| | 44 | Tax (see instrs). Check if any tax is from: a ☐ Form(s) 8814 b ☐ Form 4972 | 44 | 543. |
| | 45 | Alternative minimum tax (see instructions). Attach Form 6251 | 45 | |
| | 46 | Add lines 44 and 45 ► | 46 | 543. |
| | 47 | Foreign tax credit. Attach Form 1116 if required | 47 | | |
| | 48 | Credit for child and dependent care expenses. Attach Form 2441 | 48 | | |
| | 49 | Credit for the elderly or the disabled. Attach Schedule R | 49 | | |
| | 50 | Education credits. Attach Form 8863 | 50 | | |
| | 51 | Retirement savings contributions credit. Attach Form 8880 | 51 | | |
| | 52 | Residential energy credits. Attach Form 5695 | 52 | | |
| | 53 | Child tax credit (see instructions). Attach Form 8901 if required | 53 | | |
| | 54 | Credits from: a ☐ Form 8396 b ☐ Form 8839 c ☐ Form 8859 | 54 | | |
| | 55 | Other credits. Check applicable box(es): a ☐ Form 3800 b ☐ Form 8801 c ☐ Form | 55 | | |
| | 56 | Add lines 47 through 55. These are your total credits | 56 | |
| | 57 | Subtract line 56 from line 46. If line 56 is more than line 46, enter -0- ► | 57 | 543. |
| **Other Taxes** | 58 | Self-employment tax. Attach Schedule SE | 58 | |
| | 59 | Social security and Medicare tax on tip income not reported to employer. Attach Form 4137 | 59 | |
| | 60 | Additional tax on IRAs, other qualified retirement plans, etc. Attach Form 5329 if required | 60 | |
| | 61 | Advance earned income credit payments from Form(s) W-2, box 9 | 61 | |
| | 62 | Household employment taxes. Attach Schedule H | 62 | |
| | 63 | Add lines 57-62. This is your total tax | 63 | 543. |
| **Payments** If you have a qualifying child, attach Schedule EIC. | 64 | Federal income tax withheld from Forms W-2 and 1099 | 64 | 800. | |
| | 65 | 2006 estimated tax payments and amount applied from 2005 return | 65 | | |
| | 66a | Earned income credit (EIC) | 66a | | |
| | b | Nontaxable combat pay election ► 66b | | | |
| | 67 | Excess social security and tier 1 RRTA tax withheld (see instructions) | 67 | | |
| | 68 | Additional child tax credit. Attach Form 8812 | 68 | | |
| | 69 | Amount paid with request for extension to file (see instructions) | 69 | | |
| | 70 | Payments from: a ☐ Form 2439 b ☐ Form 4136 c ☐ Form 8885 | 70 | | |
| | 71 | Credit for federal telephone excise tax paid. Attach Form 8913 if required | 71 | 40. | |
| | 72 | Add lines 64, 65, 66a, and 67 through 71. These are your total payments ► | 72 | 840. |
| **Refund** Direct deposit? See instructions and fill in 74b, 74c, and 74d or Form 8888. | 73 | If line 72 is more than line 63, subtract line 63 from line 72. This is the amount you overpaid | 73 | 297. |
| | 74a | Amount of line 73 you want refunded to you. If Form 8888 is attached, check here ► ☐ | 74a | 297. |
| | b | Routing number XXXXXXXX ► c Type: ☐ Checking ☐ Savings d Account number XXXXXXXXXXXXXXX | | |
| | 75 | Amount of line 73 you want applied to your 2007 estimated tax ► 75 | | |
| **Amount You Owe** | 76 | Amount you owe. Subtract line 72 from line 63. For details on how to pay, see instructions ► | 76 | |
| | 77 | Estimated tax penalty (see instructions) 77 | | |
| **Third Party Designee** | | Do you want to allow another person to discuss this return with the IRS (see instructions)? ☐ Yes. Complete the following. ☒ No. Designee's name ► Phone no. ► Personal identification number (PIN) ► | | |

**Sign Here** Joint return? See instructions. Keep a copy for your records.

Under penalties of perjury, I declare that I have examined this return and accompanying schedules and statements, and to the best of my knowledge and belief, they are true, correct, and complete. Declaration of preparer (other than taxpayer) is based on all information of which preparer has any knowledge.

| Your signature ► | Date | Your occupation REC GAMBLER | Daytime phone number |
|---|---|---|---|
| Spouse's signature. If a joint return, both must sign. ► | Date | Spouse's occupation REC GAMBLER | |

| **Paid Preparer's Use Only** | Preparer's signature ► Shin-Chi Chien, EA | Date 08/07/2007 | Check if self-employed ☐ | Preparer's SSN or PTIN P00039748 |
|---|---|---|---|---|
| | Firm's name (or yours if self-employed), address, and ZIP code ► ADVANTAGE TAX PLUS 2649 W. HORIZON RIDGE PKWY #120 HENDERSON NV 89052 | | EIN 30-0003336 Phone no. (702) 207-1040 | |

Form **1040** (2006)

gross gambling winnings❸ are "canceled out" by the deducted gambling losses❺ and that amount is not included in their taxable income.

## Appendix B2-continued
# Schedule A *(Itemized)*

| SCHEDULE A (Form 1040) | Itemized Deductions | | | | OMB No. 1545-0074 |
|---|---|---|---|---|---|
| Department of the Treasury<br>Internal Revenue Service (99) | ► Attach to Form 1040.<br>► See Instructions for Schedule A (Form 1040). | | | | **2006**<br>Attachment<br>Sequence No. **07** |

Name(s) shown on Form 1040: JEAN & BRAD SCOTT    Your social security number: 123-45-6789

| | | | | | |
|---|---|---|---|---|---|
| **Medical and Dental Expenses** | **Caution.** Do not include expenses reimbursed or paid by others. | | | | |
| | 1 | Medical and dental expenses (see instructions) | 1 | | |
| | 2 | Enter amount from Form 1040, line 38 ... | 2 | | |
| | 3 | Multiply line 2 by 7.5% (.075) | 3 | | |
| | 4 | Subtract line 3 from line 1. If line 3 is more than line 1, enter -0- | | 4 | |
| **Taxes You Paid**<br><br>(See instructions.) | 5 | State and local income taxes ...............ST | 5 | 999. | |
| | 6 | Real estate taxes (see instructions) | 6 | 2,000. | |
| | 7 | Personal property taxes | 7 | 500. | |
| | 8 | Other taxes. List type and amount ► _____ | 8 | | |
| | 9 | Add lines 5 through 8 | | 9 | 3,499. |
| **Interest You Paid**<br><br>(See instructions.)<br><br>**Note.** Personal interest is not deductible. | 10 | Home mtg interest and points reported to you on Form 1098 | 10 | 10,000. | |
| | 11 | Home mortgage interest not reported to you on Form 1098. If paid to the person from whom you bought the home, see instructions and show that person's name, identifying number, and address ► | 11 | | |
| | 12 | Points not reported to you on Form 1098. See instrs for spcl rules | 12 | | |
| | 13 | Investment interest. Attach Form 4952 if required. (See instrs.) | 13 | | |
| | 14 | Add lines 10 through 13 | | 14 | 10,000. |
| **Gifts to Charity**<br><br>If you made a gift and got a benefit for it, see instructions. | 15 | Gifts by cash or check. If you made any gift of $250 or more, see instrs | 15 | 500. | |
| | 16 | Other than by cash or check. If any gift of $250 or more, see instructions. You **must** attach Form 8283 if over $500 | 16 | | |
| | 17 | Carryover from prior year | 17 | | |
| | 18 | Add lines 15 through 17 | | 18 | 500. |
| **Casualty and Theft Losses** | 19 | Casualty or theft loss(es). Attach Form 4684. (See instructions.) | | 19 | |
| **Job Expenses and Certain Miscellaneous Deductions**<br><br>(See instructions.) | 20 | Unreimbursed employee expenses – job travel, union dues, job education, etc. Attach Form 2106 or 2106-EZ if required. (See instructions.) ► | 20 | | |
| | 21 | Tax preparation fees | 21 | | |
| | 22 | Other expenses – investment, safe deposit box, etc. List type and amount ► | 22 | | |
| | 23 | Add lines 20 through 22 | 23 | | |
| | 24 | Enter amount from Form 1040, line 38 ... 24 | | | |
| | 25 | Multiply line 24 by 2% (.02) | 25 | | |
| | 26 | Subtract line 25 from line 23. If line 25 is more than line 23, enter -0- | | 26 | |
| **Other Miscellaneous Deductions** | 27 | Other – from list in the instructions. List type and amount ► GAMBLING LOSSES ❹ 60,000. | | 27 | 50,000. ❺ |
| **Total Itemized Deductions** | 28 | Is Form 1040, line 38, over $150,500 (over $75,250 if married filing separately)?<br>[X] **No.** Your deduction is not limited. Add the amounts in the far right column for lines 4 through 27. Also, enter this amount on Form 1040, line 40.<br>[ ] **Yes.** Your deduction may be limited. See instructions for the amount to enter. | | ► 28 | 63,999. |
| | 29 | If you elect to itemize deductions even though they are less than your standard deduction, check here ► [ ] | | | |

BAA For Paperwork Reduction Act Notice, see Form 1040 instructions.    FDIA0301  11/07/06    Schedule A (Form 1040) 2006

Although total gambling losses were $60,000❹, you can claim only $50,000❺, since you can count losses only up to the amount of the winnings.

## Form 1040 *side 1*

| | | | | |
|---|---|---|---|---|
| Form **1040** | Department of the Treasury — Internal Revenue Service<br>**U.S. Individual Income Tax Return** | **2006** | (99) | IRS Use Only — Do not write or staple in this space. |

For the year Jan 1 - Dec 31, 2006, or other tax year beginning , 2006, ending , 20 — OMB No. 1545-0074

**Label** (See instructions.)

Your first name MI Last name — **JEAN** SCOTT — Your social security number: **123-45-6789**

**Use the IRS label.** Otherwise, please print or type.

If a joint return, spouse's first name MI Last name — **BRAD** SCOTT — Spouse's social security number: **234-56-7891**

Home address (number and street). If you have a P.O. box, see instructions. Apartment no. — **123 MAIN STREET**

You **must** enter your social security number(s) above. ▲

City, town or post office. If you have a foreign address, see instructions. State ZIP code — **LAS VEGAS** NV **89102**

Checking a box below will not change your tax or refund.

**Presidential Election Campaign** ▶ Check here if you, or your spouse if filing jointly, want $3 to go to this fund? (see instructions) ........ ▶ ☐ You ☐ Spouse

**Filing Status**
Check only one box.

1 ☐ Single
2 ☒ Married filing jointly (even if only one had income)
3 ☐ Married filing separately. Enter spouse's SSN above & full name here ..
4 ☐ Head of household (with qualifying person). (See instructions.) If the qualifying person is a child but not your dependent, enter this child's name here ▶
5 ☐ Qualifying widow(er) with dependent child (see instructions)

**Exemptions**

6a ☒ Yourself. If someone can claim you as a dependent, **do not** check box 6a ...........
b ☒ Spouse ............................................

Boxes checked on 6a and 6b: **2**

| c Dependents: | (2) Dependent's social security number | (3) Dependent's relationship to you | (4) ✓ qualifying child for child tax credit (see instrs) |
|---|---|---|---|
| (1) First name    Last name | | | ☐ |
| | | | ☐ |
| | | | ☐ |
| | | | ☐ |

No. of children on 6c who:
• lived with you ...
• did not live with you due to divorce or separation (see instrs)

Dependents on 6c not entered above

If more than four dependents, see instructions.

d Total number of exemptions claimed ..................... Add numbers on lines above ▶ **2**

**Income**

Attach Form(s) W-2 here. Also attach Forms W-2G and 1099-R if tax was withheld.

If you did not get a W-2, see instructions.

Enclose, but do not attach, any payment. Also, please use Form 1040-V.

| | | | |
|---|---|---|---|
| 7 | Wages, salaries, tips, etc. Attach Form(s) W-2 ......... | 7 | |
| 8a | Taxable interest. Attach Schedule B if required ......... | 8a | 2,500. |
| b | Tax-exempt interest. Do not include on line 8a ...... 8b | | |
| 9a | Ordinary dividends. Attach Schedule B if required ......... | 9a | |
| b | Qualified dividends (see instrs) ............. 9b | | |
| 10 | Taxable refunds, credits, or offsets of state and local income taxes (see instructions) | 10 | |
| 11 | Alimony received ............................... | 11 | |
| 12 | Business income or (loss). Attach Schedule C or C-EZ ......... | 12 | 47,600. |
| 13 | Capital gain or (loss). Att Sch D if reqd. If not reqd, ck here ..... ▶ ☐ | 13 | |
| 14 | Other gains or (losses). Attach Form 4797 ......... | 14 | |
| 15a | IRA distributions ......... 15a | b Taxable amount (see instrs) | 15b | |
| 16a | Pensions and annuities .... 16a | b Taxable amount (see instrs) | 16b | |
| 17 | Rental real estate, royalties, partnerships, S corporations, trusts, etc. Attach Schedule E | 17 | |
| 18 | Farm income or (loss). Attach Schedule F ......... | 18 | |
| 19 | Unemployment compensation ......... | 19 | |
| 20a | Social security benefits ......... 20a | b Taxable amount (see instrs) | 20b | |
| 21 | Other income ......... | 21 | |
| 22 | Add the amounts in the far right column for lines 7 through 21. This is your **total income** ▶ | 22 | 50,100. |

**Adjusted Gross Income**

| | | | |
|---|---|---|---|
| 23 | Archer MSA deduction. Attach Form 8853 ......... 23 | | |
| 24 | Certain business expenses of reservists, performing artists, and fee-basis government officials. Attach Form 2106 or 2106-EZ ......... 24 | | |
| 25 | Health savings account deduction. Attach Form 8889 ......... 25 | | |
| 26 | Moving expenses. Attach Form 3903 ......... 26 | | |
| 27 | One-half of self-employment tax. Attach Schedule SE ......... 27 ⑩ 3,363. | | |
| 28 | Self-employed SEP, SIMPLE, and qualified plans ......... 28 ⑨ 23,847. | | |
| 29 | Self-employed health insurance deduction (see instructions) ......... 29 ❽ 2,000. | | |
| 30 | Penalty on early withdrawal of savings ......... 30 | | |
| 31a | Alimony paid  b Recipient's SSN ... ▶ 31a | | |
| 32 | IRA deduction (see instructions) ......... 32 | | |
| 33 | Student loan interest deduction (see instructions) ......... 33 | | |
| 34 | Jury duty pay you gave to your employer ......... 34 | | |
| 35 | Domestic production activities deduction. Attach Form 8903 ......... 35 | | |
| 36 | Add lines 23 - 31a and 32 - 35 ......... | 36 | 29,210. |
| 37 | Subtract line 36 from line 22. This is your **adjusted gross income** ▶ | 37 | 20,890. |

**BAA For Disclosure, Privacy Act, and Paperwork Reduction Act Notice, see instructions.** FDIA0112 11/07/06 Form **1040** (2006)

As a professional gambler, gambling winnings❻ and losses❼ are reported on Schedule C. Also note that as a professional gambler, deductions can be made for

## Appendix B3-continued
# Form 1040 *side 2*

| Form **1040** (2006) | JEAN & BRAD SCOTT | | 123-45-6789 | Page **2** |
|---|---|---|---|---|

**Tax and Credits**

| | | | |
|---|---|---|---|
| 38 | Amount from line 37 (adjusted gross income) | 38 | 20,890. |
| 39a | Check if: ☐ You were born before January 2, 1942, ☐ Blind. ☐ Spouse was born before January 2, 1942, ☐ Blind. **Total boxes checked** ▶ 39a | | |
| | b If your spouse itemizes on a separate return, or you were a dual-status alien, see instrs and ck here ▶ 39b | | |
| 40 | Itemized deductions (from Schedule A) or your **standard deduction** (see left margin) | 40 | 13,508. |
| 41 | Subtract line 40 from line 38 | 41 | 7,382. |
| 42 | If line 38 is over $112,875, or you provided housing to a person displaced by Hurricane Katrina, see instructions. Otherwise, multiply $3,300 by the total number of exemptions claimed on line 6d | 42 | 6,600. |
| 43 | Taxable income. Subtract line 42 from line 41. If line 42 is more than line 41, enter -0- | 43 | 782. |
| 44 | Tax (see instrs). Check if any tax is from: a ☐ Form(s) 8814 b ☐ Form 4972 | 44 | 79. |
| 45 | Alternative minimum tax (see instructions). Attach Form 6251 | 45 | |
| 46 | Add lines 44 and 45 ▶ | 46 | 79. |
| 47 | Foreign tax credit. Attach Form 1116 if required | 47 | |
| 48 | Credit for child and dependent care expenses. Attach Form 2441 | 48 | |
| 49 | Credit for the elderly or the disabled. Attach Schedule R | 49 | |
| 50 | Education credits. Attach Form 8863 | 50 | |
| 51 | Retirement savings contributions credit. Attach Form 8880 | 51 | |
| 52 | Residential energy credits. Attach Form 5695 | 52 | |
| 53 | Child tax credit (see instructions). Attach Form 8901 if required | 53 | |
| 54 | Credits from: a ☐ Form 8396 b ☐ Form 8839 c ☐ Form 8859 | 54 | |
| 55 | Other credits. Check applicable box(es): a ☐ Form 3800 b ☐ Form 8801 c ☐ Form | 55 | |
| 56 | Add lines 47 through 55. These are your **total credits** | 56 | |
| 57 | Subtract line 56 from line 46. If line 56 is more than line 46, enter -0- ▶ | 57 | 79. |

**Other Taxes**

| | | | |
|---|---|---|---|
| 58 | Self-employment tax. Attach Schedule SE | 58 | 6,726. |
| 59 | Social security and Medicare tax on tip income not reported to employer. Attach Form 4137 | 59 | |
| 60 | Additional tax on IRAs, other qualified retirement plans, etc. Attach Form 5329 if required | 60 | |
| 61 | Advance earned income credit payments from Form(s) W-2, box 9 | 61 | |
| 62 | Household employment taxes. Attach Schedule H | 62 | |
| 63 | Add lines 57-62. This is your total tax ▶ | 63 | 6,805. |

**Payments**

If you have a qualifying child, attach Schedule EIC.

| | | | | |
|---|---|---|---|---|
| 64 | Federal income tax withheld from Forms W-2 and 1099 | 64 | 800. | |
| 65 | 2006 estimated tax payments and amount applied from 2005 return | 65 | | |
| 66a | Earned income credit (EIC) | 66a | | |
| | b Nontaxable combat pay election ▶ 66b | | | |
| 67 | Excess social security and tier 1 RRTA tax withheld (see instructions) | 67 | | |
| 68 | Additional child tax credit. Attach Form 8812 | 68 | | |
| 69 | Amount paid with request for extension to file (see instructions) | 69 | | |
| 70 | Payments from: a ☐ Form 2439 b ☐ Form 4136 c ☐ Form 8885 | 70 | | |
| 71 | Credit for federal telephone excise tax paid. Attach Form 8913 if required | 71 | 40. | |
| 72 | Add lines 64, 65, 66a, and 67 through 71. These are your **total payments** ▶ | 72 | | 840. |

**Refund**

Direct deposit? See instructions and fill in 74b, 74c, and 74d or Form 8888.

| | | | |
|---|---|---|---|
| 73 | If line 72 is more than line 63, subtract line 63 from line 72. This is the amount you **overpaid** | 73 | |
| 74a | Amount of line 73 you want **refunded to you.** If Form 8888 is attached, check here ▶ ☐ | 74a | |
| | ▶ b Routing number ⋯ ▶ c Type: ☐ Checking ☐ Savings | | |
| | ▶ d Account number | | |
| 75 | Amount of line 73 you want applied to your 2007 estimated tax ▶ | 75 | |

**Amount You Owe**

| | | | |
|---|---|---|---|
| 76 | **Amount you owe.** Subtract line 72 from line 63. For details on how to pay, see instructions ▶ | 76 | 6,245. |
| 77 | Estimated tax penalty (see instructions) | 77 | 280. |

**Third Party Designee**

Do you want to allow another person to discuss this return with the IRS (see instructions)? ☐ Yes. Complete the following. ☒ No
Designee's name ▶   Phone no. ▶   Personal identification number (PIN) ▶

**Sign Here**

Joint return? See instructions. Keep a copy for your records.

Under penalties of perjury, I declare that I have examined this return and accompanying schedules and statements, and to the best of my knowledge and belief, they are true, correct, and complete. Declaration of preparer (other than taxpayer) is based on all information of which preparer has any knowledge.

| Your signature | Date | Your occupation PROFESSIONAL GAMBLER | Daytime phone number |
|---|---|---|---|
| Spouse's signature. If a joint return, **both must sign.** | Date | Spouse's occupation PROFESSIONAL GAMBLER | |

**Paid Preparer's Use Only**

| | | | |
|---|---|---|---|
| Preparer's signature ▶ Shin-Chi Chien, EA | Date 08/08/2007 | Check if self-employed ☐ | Preparer's SSN or PTIN P00039748 |
| Firm's name (or yours if self-employed) ▶ ADVANTAGE TAX PLUS | | | EIN 30-0003336 |
| address, and ZIP code  2649 W. HORIZON RIDGE PKWY #120  HENDERSON  NV  89052 | | | Phone no. (702) 207-1040 |

FDIA0112  11/07/06                Form **1040** (2006)

self-employed heath insurance[8], self-employed retirement-plan contributions[9], and one-half of self-employment tax[10]. Gambling-related expenses, such as automobile expenses[11] can also be reported on Schedule C.

## Appendix B3-continued
# Schedule A

| SCHEDULE A (Form 1040) | | Itemized Deductions | | OMB No. 1545-0074 **2006** |
|---|---|---|---|---|
| Department of the Treasury Internal Revenue Service (99) | | ▶ Attach to Form 1040. ▶ See Instructions for Schedule A (Form 1040). | | Attachment Sequence No. **07** |

Name(s) shown on Form 1040: **JEAN & BRAD SCOTT**

Your social security number: **123-45-6789**

| | | | | | |
|---|---|---|---|---|---|
| **Medical and Dental Expenses** | | **Caution.** Do not include expenses reimbursed or paid by others. | | | |
| | 1 | Medical and dental expenses (see instructions) | 1 | 0. | |
| | 2 | Enter amount from Form 1040, line 38 .... **2** | 20,890. | | |
| | 3 | Multiply line 2 by 7.5% (.075) | 3 | 1,567. | |
| | 4 | Subtract line 3 from line 1. If line 3 is more than line 1, enter -0- | | **4** | 0. |
| **Taxes You Paid** (See instructions.) | 5 | State and local income taxes .............ST | 5 | 508. | |
| | 6 | Real estate taxes (see instructions) | 6 | 2,000. | |
| | 7 | Personal property taxes | 7 | 500. | |
| | 8 | Other taxes. List type and amount ▶ _ _ _ _ _ _ _ _ _ _ | 8 | | |
| | 9 | Add lines 5 through 8 | | **9** | 3,008. |
| **Interest You Paid** (See instructions.) | 10 | Home mtg interest and points reported to you on Form 1098 | 10 | 10,000. | |
| | 11 | Home mortgage interest not reported to you on Form 1098. If paid to the person from whom you bought the home, see instructions and show that person's name, identifying number, and address ▶ _ _ _ _ _ _ _ _ _ _ _ _ _ _ _ _ _ _ _ _ _ _ _ _ _ _ _ _ _ _ _ _ _ _ _ _ _ _ _ | 11 | | |
| **Note.** Personal interest is not deductible. | 12 | Points not reported to you on Form 1098. See instrs for spcl rules | 12 | | |
| | 13 | Investment interest. Attach Form 4952 if required. (See instrs.) | 13 | | |
| | 14 | Add lines 10 through 13 | | **14** | 10,000. |
| **Gifts to Charity** If you made a gift and got a benefit for it, see instructions. | 15 | Gifts by cash or check. If you made any gift of $250 or more, see instrs | 15 | 500. | |
| | 16 | Other than by cash or check. If any gift of $250 or more, see instructions. You **must** attach Form 8283 if over $500 | 16 | | |
| | 17 | Carryover from prior year | 17 | | |
| | 18 | Add lines 15 through 17 | | **18** | 500. |
| **Casualty and Theft Losses** | 19 | Casualty or theft loss(es). Attach Form 4684. (See instructions.) | | **19** | |
| **Job Expenses and Certain Miscellaneous Deductions** (See instructions.) | 20 | Unreimbursed employee expenses — job travel, union dues, job education, etc. Attach Form 2106 or 2106-EZ if required. (See instructions.) ▶ _ _ _ _ _ _ _ _ _ _ _ _ _ _ _ _ _ _ _ _ _ _ _ _ _ | 20 | | |
| | 21 | Tax preparation fees | 21 | | |
| | 22 | Other expenses — investment, safe deposit box, etc. List type and amount ▶ _ _ _ _ _ _ _ _ _ _ _ _ _ _ _ _ | 22 | | |
| | 23 | Add lines 20 through 22 | 23 | | |
| | 24 | Enter amount from Form 1040, line 38 .... **24** | | | |
| | 25 | Multiply line 24 by 2% (.02) | 25 | | |
| | 26 | Subtract line 25 from line 23. If line 25 is more than line 23, enter -0- | | **26** | |
| **Other Miscellaneous Deductions** | 27 | Other — from list in the instructions. List type and amount ▶ _ _ _ _ _ _ _ _ _ _ _ _ _ _ _ _ _ _ _ _ | | **27** | |
| **Total Itemized Deductions** | 28 | Is Form 1040, line 38, over $150,500 (over $75,250 if married filing separately)? | | | |
| | | [X] **No.** Your deduction is not limited. Add the amounts in the far right column for lines 4 through 27. Also, enter this amount on Form 1040, line 40. | | | |
| | | [ ] **Yes.** Your deduction may be limited. See instructions for the amount to enter. | ▶ | **28** | 13,508. |
| | 29 | If you elect to itemize deductions even though they are less than your standard deduction, check here ▶ [ ] | | | |

**BAA For Paperwork Reduction Act Notice, see Form 1040 instructions.**    FDIA0301  11/07/06    Schedule **A** (Form 1040) 2006

## Appendix B3-continued
# Schedule C

| SCHEDULE C (Form 1040) | **Profit or Loss From Business** (Sole Proprietorship) | | OMB No. 1545-0074 **2006** |
|---|---|---|---|
| Department of the Treasury Internal Revenue Service (99) | ► Partnerships, joint ventures, etc., must file Form 1065 or 1065-B. ► Attach to Form 1040, 1040NR, or 1041. ► See Instructions for Schedule C (Form 1040). | | Attachment Sequence No. **09** |

Name of proprietor: JEAN SCOTT — Social security number (SSN): 123-45-6789

A Principal business or profession, including product or service (see instructions): PROFESSIONAL GAMBLER — B Enter code from instructions ►

C Business name. If no separate business name, leave blank. — D Employer ID number (EIN), if any

E Business address (including suite or room no.)► 123 MAIN STREET
City, town or post office, state, and ZIP code LAS VEGAS, NV 89102

F Accounting method: (1) [X] Cash (2) [ ] Accrual (3) [ ] Other (specify) ►

G Did you 'materially participate' in the operation of this business during 2006? If 'No,' see instructions for limit on losses ... [X] Yes [ ] No

H If you started or acquired this business during 2006, check here ► [ ]

### Part I  Income

| | | | |
|---|---|---|---|
| 1 | Gross receipts or sales. Caution. If this income was reported to you on Form W-2 and the 'Statutory employee' box on that form was checked, see the instructions and check here ► [ ] | 1 | 250,000. ❻ |
| 2 | Returns and allowances | 2 | |
| 3 | Subtract line 2 from line 1 | 3 | 250,000. |
| 4 | Cost of goods sold (from line 42 on page 2) | 4 | |
| 5 | Gross profit. Subtract line 4 from line 3 | 5 | 250,000. |
| 6 | Other income, including federal and state gasoline or fuel tax credit or refund | 6 | |
| 7 | Gross income. Add lines 5 and 6 ► | 7 | 250,000. |

### Part II  Expenses. Enter expenses for business use of your home only on line 30.

| | | | | | |
|---|---|---|---|---|---|
| 8 | Advertising | 8 | 18 Office expense | 18 | |
| 9 | Car and truck expenses (see instructions) | 9 ❶ 2,000. | 19 Pension and profit-sharing plans | 19 | |
| 10 | Commissions and fees | 10 | 20 Rent or lease (see instructions): | | |
| 11 | Contract labor (see instructions) | 11 | a Vehicles, machinery, and equipment | 20a | |
| 12 | Depletion | 12 | b Other business property | 20b | |
| 13 | Depreciation and section 179 expense deduction (not included in Part III) (see instructions) | 13 | 21 Repairs and maintenance | 21 | |
| | | | 22 Supplies (not included in Part III) | 22 | |
| | | | 23 Taxes and licenses | 23 | |
| 14 | Employee benefit programs (other than on line 19) | 14 | 24 Travel, meals, and entertainment: | | |
| 15 | Insurance (other than health) | 15 | a Travel | 24a | |
| 16 | Interest: | | b Deductible meals and entertainment | 24b | |
| a | Mortgage (paid to banks, etc) | 16a | 25 Utilities | 25 | |
| b | Other | 16b | 26 Wages (less employment credits) | 26 | |
| 17 | Legal & professional services | 17 250. | 27 Other expenses (from line 48 on page 2) | 27 | 200,150. |
| 28 | Total expenses before expenses for business use of home. Add lines 8 through 27 in columns ► | | | 28 | 202,400. |

29 Tentative profit (loss). Subtract line 28 from line 7 — 29 | 47,600.

30 Expenses for business use of your home. Attach Form 8829 — 30

31 Net profit or (loss). Subtract line 30 from line 29.
- If a profit, enter on both Form 1040, line 12, and Schedule SE, line 2 or on Form 1040NR, line 13 (statutory employees, see instructions). Estates and trusts, enter on Form 1041, line 3.
- If a loss, you must go to line 32. — 31 | 47,600.

32 If you have a loss, check the box that describes your investment in this activity (see instructions).
- If you checked 32a, enter the loss on both Form 1040, line 12, and Schedule SE, line 2, or on Form 1040NR, line 13 (statutory employees, see instructions). Estates and trusts, enter on Form 1041, line 3. — 32a [ ] All investment is at risk.
- If you checked 32b, you must attach Form 6198. Your loss may be limited. — 32b [ ] Some investment is not at risk.

BAA For Paperwork Reduction Act Notice, see Form 1040 instructions. — Schedule C (Form 1040) 2006

FDIZ0112  11/03/06

## Appendix B3-continued
# Schedule C *side 2*

Schedule **C** (Form 1040) 2006  JEAN SCOTT                    123-45-6789      Page 2

**Part III**    **Cost of Goods Sold** (see instructions)

33  Method(s) used to value closing inventory:  **a** ☐ Cost  **b** ☐ Lower of cost or market  **c** ☐ Other (attach explanation)

34  Was there any change in determining quantities, costs, or valuations between opening and closing inventory?
If 'Yes,' attach explanation ........................................................................................ ☐ Yes  ☐ No

| | | |
|---|---|---|
| 35 Inventory at beginning of year. If different from last year's closing inventory, attach explanation .................................................................. | **35** | |
| 36 Purchases less cost of items withdrawn for personal use ........................................ | **36** | |
| 37 Cost of labor. Do not include any amounts paid to yourself ...................................... | **37** | |
| 38 Materials and supplies ....................................................................... | **38** | |
| 39 Other costs ................................................................................ | **39** | |
| 40 Add lines 35 through 39 ...................................................................... | **40** | |
| 41 Inventory at end of year ...................................................................... | **41** | |
| 42 **Cost of goods sold.** Subtract line 41 from line 40. Enter the result here and on page 1, line 4 ......... | **42** | |

**Part IV**    **Information on Your Vehicle.** Complete this part **only** if you are claiming car or truck expenses on line 9 and are not required to file Form 4562 for this business. See the instructions for line 13 to find out if you must file Form 4562.

43  When did you place your vehicle in service for business purposes? (month, day, year)  ► _ _ _ _ _ _ _ _ _ _ _ .

44  Of the total number of miles you drove your vehicle during 2006, enter the number of miles you used your vehicle for:
**a** Business _ _ _ _ _ _ _ _ _ _ _  **b** Commuting (see instructions) _ _ _ _ _ _ _ _ _ _ _  **c** Other _ _ _ _ _ _ _ _ _ _ _

45  Do you (or your spouse) have another vehicle available for personal use? ..................................... ☐ Yes  ☐ No

46  Was your vehicle available for personal use during off-duty hours? ........................................... ☐ Yes  ☐ No

**47a** Do you have evidence to support your deduction? ........................................................... ☐ Yes  ☐ No

**b** If 'Yes,' is the evidence written? ........................................................................ ☐ Yes  ☐ No

**Part V**    **Other Expenses.** List below business expenses not included on lines 8-26 or line 30.

| | |
|---|---|
| BOOKS, EDUCATIONAL MATERIALS _ _ _ _ _ _ _ _ _ _ _ _ _ _ _ _ _ _ _ _ _ _ _ _ _ _ _ _ _ _ | 150. |
| FULLY DOCUMENTED GAMBLING LOSSES PER REV PROC 77-29 _ _ _ _ _ _ _ _ _ _ _ _ _ _ | 200,000. ❼ |
| _ _ _ _ _ _ _ _ _ _ _ _ _ _ _ _ _ _ _ _ _ _ _ _ _ _ _ _ _ _ _ _ _ _ _ _ _ _ | |
| _ _ _ _ _ _ _ _ _ _ _ _ _ _ _ _ _ _ _ _ _ _ _ _ _ _ _ _ _ _ _ _ _ _ _ _ _ _ | |
| _ _ _ _ _ _ _ _ _ _ _ _ _ _ _ _ _ _ _ _ _ _ _ _ _ _ _ _ _ _ _ _ _ _ _ _ _ _ | |
| _ _ _ _ _ _ _ _ _ _ _ _ _ _ _ _ _ _ _ _ _ _ _ _ _ _ _ _ _ _ _ _ _ _ _ _ _ _ | |
| _ _ _ _ _ _ _ _ _ _ _ _ _ _ _ _ _ _ _ _ _ _ _ _ _ _ _ _ _ _ _ _ _ _ _ _ _ _ | |
| **48 Total other expenses.** Enter here and on page 1, line 27 ....................  **48** | 200,150. |

Schedule **C** (Form 1040) 2006

FDIZ0112  11/03/06

## Appendix B3-continued
# Schedule SE

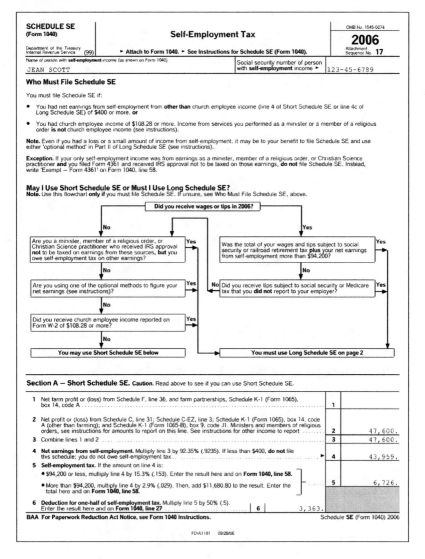

Note that the full amount of SE tax from line 5 above must be carried over to line 58 on page 2 of the return, but half of that figure (from line 6 above) is put on page 1 of the return as a deduction on line 27.[10]

# State and Federal Tax Forms for Indiana Residents

## Form 1040

| Form **1040** | Department of the Treasury — Internal Revenue Service<br>**U.S. Individual Income Tax Return** **2006** | (99) | IRS Use Only — Do not write or staple in this space. |
|---|---|---|---|

For the year Jan 1 - Dec 31, 2006, or other tax year beginning _____ , 2006, ending _____ , 20 _____     OMB No. 1545-0074

**Label** (See instructions.)

Your first name: JEAN   MI   Last name: SCOTT    Your social security number: 123-45-6789

**Use the IRS label.** Otherwise, please print or type.

If a joint return, spouse's first name: BRAD   MI   Last name: SCOTT    Spouse's social security number: 234-56-7891

Home address (number and street). If you have a P.O. box, see instructions: 123 MAIN STREET    Apartment no.

You **must** enter your social security number(s) above. ▲

City, town or post office. If you have a foreign address, see instructions: LAS VEGAS   State NV   ZIP code 89102

Checking a box below will not change your tax or refund.

**Presidential Election Campaign** ► Check here if you, or your spouse if filing jointly, want $3 to go to this fund? (see instructions) . . . . . . . . ► ☐ You ☐ Spouse

**Filing Status**
Check only one box.

1 ☐ Single
2 ☒ Married filing jointly (even if only one had income)
3 ☐ Married filing separately. Enter spouse's SSN above & full name here ►
4 ☐ Head of household (with qualifying person). (See instructions.) If the qualifying person is a child but not your dependent, enter this child's name here ►
5 ☐ Qualifying widow(er) with dependent child (see instructions)

**Exemptions**

6a ☒ Yourself. If someone can claim you as a dependent, **do not** check box 6a . . . . . . . . . . }
b ☒ Spouse . . . . . . . . . . . . . . . . . . . . . . . . . . . . . . . . . . . . . . . . . }

Boxes checked on 6a and 6b: **2**

c Dependents:

| (1) First name   Last name | (2) Dependent's social security number | (3) Dependent's relationship to you | (4) ✓ if qualifying child for child tax credit (see instrs) |
|---|---|---|---|
| | | | ☐ |
| | | | ☐ |
| | | | ☐ |
| | | | ☐ |

No. of children on 6c who:
• lived with you . . . . .
• did not live with you due to divorce or separation (see instrs) . . .
Dependents on 6c not entered above . . .

If more than four dependents, see instructions.

d Total number of exemptions claimed . . . . . . . . . . . . . . . . . . . . . . . . . . . . . . . . . . .

Add numbers on lines above ► **2**

**Income**

Attach Form(s) W-2 here. Also attach Forms W-2G and 1099-R if tax was withheld.

If you did not get a W-2, see instructions.

Enclose, but do not attach, any payment. Also, please use Form 1040-V.

| | | |
|---|---|---|
| 7 Wages, salaries, tips, etc. Attach Form(s) W-2 . . . . . . . . . . . . . . . . . . . . . ► | 7 | 25,000. |
| 8a Taxable interest. Attach Schedule B if required . . . . . . . . . . . . . . . . . . . . | 8a | 1,000. |
| b Tax-exempt interest. **Do not** include on line 8a . . . . . . . | 8b | |
| 9a Ordinary dividends. Attach Schedule B if required . . . . . . . . . . . . . . . . . . | 9a | |
| b Qualified dividends (see instrs) . . . . . . . . . . . . . . . . | 9b | |
| 10 Taxable refunds, credits, or offsets of state and local income taxes (see instructions) . . . . . . . . . . . . | 10 | |
| 11 Alimony received . . . . . . . . . . . . . . . . . . . . . . . . . . . . . . . . . . | 11 | |
| 12 Business income or (loss). Attach Schedule C or C-EZ . . . . . . . . . . . . . . . . | 12 | |
| 13 Capital gain or (loss). Att Sch D if reqd. If not reqd, ck here . . . . . . . . . . . ► ☐ | 13 | |
| 14 Other gains or (losses). Attach Form 4797 . . . . . . . . . . . . . . . . . . . . . | 14 | |
| 15a IRA distributions . . . . . . . . 15a | b Taxable amount (see instrs) | 15b | |
| 16a Pensions and annuities . . . . 16a | b Taxable amount (see instrs) | 16b | |
| 17 Rental real estate, royalties, partnerships, S corporations, trusts, etc. Attach Schedule E . . . | 17 | |
| 18 Farm income or (loss). Attach Schedule F . . . . . . . . . . . . . . . . . . . . . | 18 | |
| 19 Unemployment compensation . . . . . . . . . . . . . . . . . . . . . . . . . . . | 19 | |
| 20a Social security benefits . . . . 20a | b Taxable amount (see instrs) | 20b | |
| 21 Other income GAMBLING WINNINGS | 21 | 50,000. |
| 22 Add the amounts in the far right column for lines 7 through 21. This is your **total income** ► | 22 | 76,000. |

**Adjusted Gross Income**

| | | |
|---|---|---|
| 23 Archer MSA deduction. Attach Form 8853 . . . . | 23 | |
| 24 Certain business expenses of reservists, performing artists, and fee-basis government officials. Attach Form 2106 or 2106-EZ . . . . | 24 | |
| 25 Health savings account deduction. Attach Form 8889 . . . . | 25 | |
| 26 Moving expenses. Attach Form 3903 . . . . | 26 | |
| 27 One-half of self-employment tax. Attach Schedule SE . . . . . | 27 | |
| 28 Self-employed SEP, SIMPLE, and qualified plans . . . . | 28 | |
| 29 Self-employed health insurance deduction (see instructions) . . . . . . . | 29 | |
| 30 Penalty on early withdrawal of savings . . . . . . . . . . | 30 | |
| 31a Alimony paid b Recipient's SSN . . . . ► | 31a | |
| 32 IRA deduction (see instructions) . . . . . . . . . . | 32 | |
| 33 Student loan interest deduction (see instructions) . . . . | 33 | |
| 34 Jury duty pay you gave to your employer . . . . . . . . . | 34 | |
| 35 Domestic production activities deduction. Attach Form 8903 . . . . . . . | 35 | |
| 36 Add lines 23 - 31a and 32 - 35 . . . . . . . . . . . . . . . . . . . . . . . . . ► | 36 | |
| 37 Subtract line 36 from line 22. This is your **adjusted gross income** . . . . . . . . . . . . ► | 37 | 76,000. 🄬 |

**BAA For Disclosure, Privacy Act, and Paperwork Reduction Act Notice, see instructions.**    FDIA0112 11/07/06    Form **1040** (2006)

Notice you must carry over the adjusted gross income (AGI) figure🄬 from

## Appendix B4-continued
# Form 1040 *side 2*

| Form **1040** (2006) | JEAN & BRAD SCOTT | | | | 123-45-6789 | | Page **2** |
|---|---|---|---|---|---|---|---|
| **Tax and Credits** | 38 | Amount from line 37 (adjusted gross income) | | | | 38 | 76,000. |
| **Standard Deduction for –** | 39a | Check if: ☐ You were born before January 2, 1942, ☐ Blind. ☐ Spouse was born before January 2, 1942, ☐ Blind. | **Total boxes checked** ▶ 39a ☐ | | | | |
| • People who checked any box on line 39a or 39b or who can be claimed as a dependent, see instructions. | b | If your spouse itemizes on a separate return, or you were a dual-status alien, see instrs and ck here ▶ 39b ☐ | | | | | |
| | 40 | **Itemized deductions** (from Schedule A) or your **standard deduction** (see left margin) | | | | 40 | 63,000. |
| | 41 | Subtract line 40 from line 38 | | | | 41 | 13,000. |
| | 42 | If line 38 is over $112,875, or you provided housing to a person displaced by Hurricane Katrina, see instructions. Otherwise, multiply $3,300 by the total number of exemptions claimed on line 6d | | | | 42 | 6,600. |
| • All others: | 43 | **Taxable income.** Subtract line 42 from line 41. If line 42 is more than line 41, enter -0- | | | | 43 | 6,400. |
| Single or Married filing separately, $5,150 | 44 | Tax (see instrs). Check if any tax is from: **a** ☐ Form(s) 8814 **b** ☐ Form 4972 | | | | 44 | 643. |
| | 45 | **Alternative minimum tax** (see instructions). Attach Form 6251 | | | | 45 | |
| Married filing jointly or Qualifying widow(er), $10,300 | 46 | Add lines 44 and 45 | | | ▶ | 46 | 643. |
| | 47 | Foreign tax credit. Attach Form 1116 if required | 47 | | | | |
| | 48 | Credit for child and dependent care expenses. Attach Form 2441 | 48 | | | | |
| Head of household, $7,550 | 49 | Credit for the elderly or the disabled. Attach Schedule R | 49 | | | | |
| | 50 | Education credits. Attach Form 8863 | 50 | | | | |
| | 51 | Retirement savings contributions credit. Attach Form 8880 | 51 | | | | |
| | 52 | Residential energy credits. Attach Form 5695 | 52 | | | | |
| | 53 | Child tax credit (see instructions). Attach Form 8901 if required | 53 | | | | |
| | 54 | Credits from: **a** ☐ Form 8396 **b** ☐ Form 8839 **c** ☐ Form 8859 | 54 | | | | |
| | 55 | Other credits. Check applicable box(es): **a** ☐ Form 3800 **b** ☐ Form 8801 **c** ☐ Form ___ | 55 | | | | |
| | 56 | Add lines 47 through 55. These are your **total credits** | | | | 56 | |
| | 57 | Subtract line 56 from line 46. If line 56 is more than line 46, enter -0- | | | ▶ | 57 | 643. |
| **Other Taxes** | 58 | Self-employment tax. Attach Schedule SE | | | | 58 | |
| | 59 | Social security and Medicare tax on tip income not reported to employer. Attach Form 4137 | | | | 59 | |
| | 60 | Additional tax on IRAs, other qualified retirement plans, etc. Attach Form 5329 if required | | | | 60 | |
| | 61 | Advance earned income credit payments from Form(s) W-2, box 9 | | | | 61 | |
| | 62 | Household employment taxes. Attach Schedule H | | | | 62 | |
| | 63 | Add lines 57-62. This is your **total tax** | | | ▶ | 63 | 643. |
| **Payments** | 64 | Federal income tax withheld from Forms W-2 and 1099 | 64 | 800. | | | |
| If you have a qualifying child, attach Schedule EIC. | 65 | 2006 estimated tax payments and amount applied from 2005 return | 65 | | | | |
| | 66a | **Earned income credit (EIC)** | 66a | | | | |
| | b | Nontaxable combat pay election ▶ 66b | | | | | |
| | 67 | Excess social security and tier 1 RRTA tax withheld (see instructions) | 67 | | | | |
| | 68 | Additional child tax credit. Attach Form 8812 | 68 | | | | |
| | 69 | Amount paid with request for extension to file (see instructions) | 69 | | | | |
| | 70 | Payments from: **a** ☐ Form 2439 **b** ☐ Form 4136 **c** ☐ Form 8885 | 70 | | | | |
| | 71 | Credit for federal telephone excise tax paid. Attach Form 8913 if required | 71 | 40. | | | |
| | 72 | Add lines 64, 65, 66a, and 67 through 71. These are your **total payments** | | | ▶ | 72 | 840. |
| **Refund** | 73 | If line 72 is more than line 63, subtract line 63 from line 72. This is the amount you **overpaid** | | | | 73 | 197. |
| Direct deposit? See instructions and fill in 74b, 74c, and 74d or Form 8888. | 74a | Amount of line 73 you want **refunded to you.** If Form 8888 is attached, check here ▶ ☐ | | | | 74a | 197. |
| | ▶ b | Routing number XXXXXXXX ▶ **c** Type: ☐ Checking ☐ Savings | | | | | |
| | ▶ d | Account number XXXXXXXXXXXXXXXXX | | | | | |
| | 75 | Amount of line 73 you want applied to your 2007 estimated tax ▶ 75 | | | | | |
| **Amount You Owe** | 76 | **Amount you owe.** Subtract line 72 from line 63. For details on how to pay, see instructions | | | ▶ | 76 | |
| | 77 | Estimated tax penalty (see instructions) | 77 | | | | |
| **Third Party Designee** | Do you want to allow another person to discuss this return with the IRS (see instructions)? ☐ Yes. Complete the following. ☒ No | | | | | | |
| | Designee's name ▶ | Phone no. ▶ | Personal identification number (PIN) ▶ | | | | |
| **Sign Here** Joint return? See instructions. Keep a copy for your records. | Under penalties of perjury, I declare that I have examined this return and accompanying schedules and statements, and to the best of my knowledge and belief, they are true, correct, and complete. Declaration of preparer (other than taxpayer) is based on all information of which preparer has any knowledge. | | | | | | |
| | Your signature ▶ | Date | Your occupation REC GAMBLER | Daytime phone number | | | |
| | Spouse's signature. If a joint return, **both** must sign. ▶ | Date | Spouse's occupation REC GAMBLER | | | | |
| **Paid Preparer's Use Only** | Preparer's signature ▶ Shin-Chi Chien, EA | Date 08/07/2007 | Check if self-employed ☐ | Preparer's SSN or PTIN P00039748 | | | |
| | Firm's name (or yours if self-employed), address, and ZIP code ▶ ADVANTAGE TAX PLUS 2649 W. HORIZON RIDGE PKWY #120 HENDERSON NV 89052 | | EIN 30-0003336 Phone no. (702) 207-1040 | | | | |
| | FDIA0112 11/07/06 | | | | | Form **1040** (2006) | |

line 37 of your federal tax return to line 1 of your Indiana return. That figure included your *gross* winnings. But there is no place to deduct your gambling losses ⓭ on the Indiana Schedule 1 as you did on the federal Schedule A. Gambling losses are not deductible for Indiana filers. Therefore, these taxpayers will have to pay

## Appendix B4-continued
# Schedule A

**SCHEDULE A (Form 1040)** — Department of the Treasury, Internal Revenue Service (99)

**Itemized Deductions** ► Attach to Form 1040. ► See Instructions for Schedule A (Form 1040).

OMB No. 1545-0074 — **2006** — Attachment Sequence No. **07**

Name(s) shown on Form 1040: **JEAN & BRAD SCOTT** — Your social security number: **123-45-6789**

**Medical and Dental Expenses**
Caution. Do not include expenses reimbursed or paid by others.
1 Medical and dental expenses (see instructions) — 1
2 Enter amount from Form 1040, line 38 — 2
3 Multiply line 2 by 7.5% (.075) — 3
4 Subtract line 3 from line 1. If line 3 is more than line 1, enter -0- — **4**

**Taxes You Paid** (See instructions.)
5 State and local income taxes — 5
6 Real estate taxes (see instructions) — 6 — 2,000.
7 Personal property taxes — 7 — 500.
8 Other taxes. List type and amount ► — 8
9 Add lines 5 through 8 — **9** — 2,500.

**Interest You Paid** (See instructions.)
Note. Personal interest is not deductible.
10 Home mtg interest and points reported to you on Form 1098 — 10 — 10,000.
11 Home mortgage interest not reported to you on Form 1098. If paid to the person from whom you bought the home, see instructions and show that person's name, identifying number, and address ► — 11
12 Points not reported to you on Form 1098. See instrs for spcl rules — 12
13 Investment interest. Attach Form 4952 if required. (See instrs.) — 13
14 Add lines 10 through 13 — **14** — 10,000.

**Gifts to Charity**
If you made a gift and got a benefit for it, see instructions.
15 Gifts by cash or check. If you made any gift of $250 or more, see instrs — 15 — 500.
16 Other than by cash or check. If any gift of $250 or more, see instructions. You **must** attach Form 8283 if over $500 — 16
17 Carryover from prior year — 17
18 Add lines 15 through 17 — **18** — 500.

**Casualty and Theft Losses**
19 Casualty or theft loss(es). Attach Form 4684. (See instructions.) — **19**

**Job Expenses and Certain Miscellaneous Deductions** (See instructions.)
20 Unreimbursed employee expenses – job travel, union dues, job education, etc. Attach Form 2106 or 2106-EZ if required. (See instructions.) ► — 20
21 Tax preparation fees — 21
22 Other expenses – investment, safe deposit box, etc. List type and amount ► — 22
23 Add lines 20 through 22 — 23
24 Enter amount from Form 1040, line 38 — 24
25 Multiply line 24 by 2% (.02) — 25
26 Subtract line 25 from line 23. If line 25 is more than line 23, enter -0- — **26**

**Other Miscellaneous Deductions**
27 Other – from list in the instructions. List type and amount ► GAMBLING LOSSES ⓭ 60,000. — **27** — 50,000. ⓮

**Total Itemized Deductions**
28 Is Form 1040, line 38, over $150,500 (over $75,250 if married filing separately)?
☒ No. Your deduction is not limited. Add the amounts in the far right column for lines 4 through 27. Also, enter this amount on Form 1040, line 40. — ► 28 — 63,000.
☐ Yes. Your deduction may be limited. See instructions for the amount to enter.
29 If you elect to itemize deductions even though they are less than your standard deduction, check here ► ☐

BAA For Paperwork Reduction Act Notice, see Form 1040 instructions. — FDIA0301 11/07/06 — Schedule A (Form 1040) 2006

Indiana tax on the full amount of their gross winnings even though they actually had a net loss at the end of the year.

Although total gambling losses were $60,000⓭, you can claim only $50,000⓮, since you can count losses only up to the amount of the winnings.

# Appendix B4-continued
## Form IT-40 *side 1*

| Form **IT-40** State Form 154 R5/8-06 | **2006** | **Indiana Full-Year Resident Individual Income Tax Return** | **Due April 16, 2007** |
|---|---|---|---|

If you are **not** filing for the calendar year January 1 through December 31, 2006, enter period from:　　　　　　to:

```
123-45-6789        234-56-7891
JEAN               SCOTT
BRAD               SCOTT
123 MAIN STREET
            45100
```

☐ Check if applying for ITIN　　　　　☐ Check if applying for ITIN

Enter the **2-digit county code** numbers (found in the instructions) for the county where you lived and worked on January 1, 2006.　**Yourself**　　　　　　**Spouse**

Check the box if you are married filing separately ☐

| County where you lived | County where you worked | | County where spouse lived | County where spouse worked | School Corp. Number (see instructions) | | |
|---|---|---|---|---|---|---|---|

| | | | | | |
|---|---|---|---|---|---|
| 1 | Enter your federal adjusted gross income from your federal return (see instructions) | 1 | 76,000 . 00 |
| 2 | Tax add-back: certain taxes deducted from federal Schedule C, C-EZ, E, and/or F | 2 | 00 |
| 3 | Net operating loss carryforward from federal Form 1040, 'Other income' line | 3 | 00 |
| 4 | Income taxed on federal Form 4972 (lump sum distribution) (attach Form 4972; see instructions) | 4 | 00 |
| 5 | Domestic production activities add-back (see instructions) | 5 | 00 |
| 6 | Other (see instructions) | 6 | 00 |
| 7 | Add lines 1 through 6 ............................ **Total Indiana Income** ► | 7 | 76,000 . 00 |
| 8 | Indiana deductions: Enter amount from Schedule 1, line 12 and attach Schedule 1 | 8 | 2,000 . 00 |
| 9 | Line 7 minus line 8 ............................ **Indiana Adjusted Income** ► | 9 | 74,000 . 00 |
| 10 | Number of exemptions claimed on your federal return .... 2 x $1,000. (If no federal return was filed, enter $1,000 per qualifying person; see instructions.) | 10 | 2,000 . 00 |
| 11 | Additional exemption for certain dependent children (see instructions). Enter number ☐ x $1,500 | 11 | 00 |
| 12 | Check box(es) below for additional exemptions if, by December 31, 2006: **You were:** ☐ 65 or older ☐ or blind. **Spouse was:** ☐ 65 or older ☐ or blind. Total the number of boxes checked ... ☐ x $1,000 | 12 | 00 |
| 13 | Check box(es) below for additional exemptions if, by December 31, 2006: **You were:** ☐ 65 or older and line 1 above is less than $40,000. **Spouse was:** ☐ 65 or older and line 1 above is less than $40,000. Total the number of boxes checked ..... ☐ x $500 | 13 | 00 |
| 14 | Add lines 10, 11, 12 and 13 ........................ **Total Exemptions** ► | 14 | 2,000 . 00 |
| 15 | Line 9 minus line 14 (if answer is less than zero, leave blank) ........... **State Taxable Income** ► | 15 | 72,000 . 00 |
| 16 | State adjusted gross income tax: multiply line 15 by 3.4% (.034) | 16 | 2,448 . 00 |
| 17 | County income tax. See instructions | 17 | 00 |
| 18 | Use tax due on out-of-state purchases. See instructions | 18 | 00 |
| 19 | Household employment taxes: attach Schedule IN-H (see instructions) | 19 | 00 |
| 20 | Indiana advance earned income credit payments from W-2(s) (see instructions) | 20 | 00 |
| 21 | Add lines 16 through 20. Enter here and on line 31 on page 2 ............ **Total Tax** ► | 21 | 2,448 . 00 |
| 22 | Indiana state tax withheld (from box 17 of your W-2s, box 8 of WH-18s or from 1099s) | 22 | 00 |
| 23 | Indiana county tax withheld (from box 19 of your W-2s, box 9 of WH-18s or from 1099s) | 23 | 00 |
| 24 | Estimated tax paid for 2006: include any extension payment made with Form IT-9 | 24 | 00 |
| 25 | Unified tax credit for the elderly. See instructions | 25 | 00 |
| 26 | Earned income credit: attach Schedule IN-EIC and enter amount from Section A, line A-2 | 26 | 00 |
| 27 | Lake County residential income tax credit: see instructions | 27 | 00 |
| 28 | Economic development for a growing economy credit (see instructions) | 28 | 00 |
| 29 | Indiana credits: enter the total from Schedule 2, line 7 and attach Schedule 2 | 29 | 00 |
| 30 | Add lines 22 through 29. Enter here and on line 32 on page 2 ............ **Total Credits** ► | 30 | 00 |

| AA | BB | CC | DD | Turn the page ► |
|---|---|---|---|---|

1030　　　　　　　　　　　INA0512 10/26/06

*(left margin, vertical): STAPLE W-2 FORMS ON THIS PAGE ONLY BETWEEN LINES 1 AND 30*

*(right margin, vertical): PAPER CLIP CHECK/MONEY ORDER HERE*

# Appendix B4-continued
## Form IT-40 *side 2*

Form **IT-40**   JEAN & BRAD SCOTT     123-45-6789   Page **2**

| Line | Description | | Amount |
|---|---|---|---|
| 31 | Enter the Total Tax from line 21 on page 1 of this form | 31 | 2,448.00 |
| 32 | Enter the Total Credits from line 30 on page 1 of this form | 32 | 00 |
| 33 | If line 32 is more than line 31, subtract line 31 from line 32 (if smaller, skip to line 40) | 33 | 00 |
| 34 | Amount of line 33 to be donated to the Indiana Nongame Wildlife Fund (see instructions) | 34 | 00 |
| 35 | Subtract line 34 from line 33   **SUBTOTAL** | 35 | 00 |
| 36 | Amount to be applied to your 2007 estimated tax account (see instructions) | 36 | 00 |
| 37 | Penalty for underpayment of estimated tax for 2006: attach Schedule IT-2210 or IT-2210A | 37 | 220.00 |
| 38 | **Refund:** Line 35 minus lines 36 and 37 (if less than zero see instructions)   **YOUR REFUND** | 38 | 00 |

Direct Deposit
- 39a Routing Number
- b Account Number
- c Type of Account   ☐ Checking   ☐ Savings   ☐ Hoosier Works

If you want to **DIRECT DEPOSIT** your refund, see instructions.

| Line | Description | | Amount |
|---|---|---|---|
| 40 | If line 31 is more than line 32, subtract line 32 from line 31. **Add to this any amounts from lines 36 and 37, and enter total here** (see instructions)   **SUBTOTAL** | 40 | 2,668.00 |
| 41 | Penalty if filed after due date (see instructions) | 41 | 00 |
| 42 | Interest if filed after due date (see instructions) | 42 | 00 |
| 43 | **Amount Due:** Add lines 40, 41 and 42   **AMOUNT YOU OWE** | 43 | 2,668.00 |

► No payment is due if you owe less than $1. **Do Not Send Cash.** Please make your check or money order payable to: **Indiana Department of Revenue.** Credit card payers must see instructions.

**Out-of-State Income Information**
- Enter any salary, wage, tip and/or commission received from Illinois, Kentucky, Michigan, Ohio, Pennsylvania and/or Wisconsin:   Yourself $ _____   Spouse $ _____

- If two-thirds of your gross income was made from farming or fishing, please check here ☐
  **Important:** If you checked the box, you **must** attach Schedule IT-2210 or IT-2210A.

Are you filing a federal income tax return for 2006?   Yes ☒   No ☐
I authorize the department to discuss my return with my tax preparer   Yes ☐   No ☐

Your Daytime Telephone Number _____
Spouse's Daytime Telephone Number _____
E-mail address where we can reach you (see instructions) _____

**Authorization**

Under penalty of perjury, I have examined this return and all attachments and to the best of my knowledge and belief, it is true, complete and correct. I understand that if this is a joint return, any refund will be made payable to us jointly and each of us is liable for all taxes due under this return. Also, my request for direct deposit of my refund includes my authorization to the Indiana Department of Revenue (department) to furnish my financial institution with my routing number, account number, account type, and social security number to ensure my refund is properly deposited. I give permission to the department to contact the Social Security Administration in order to confirm the Social Security numbers(s) used on this return are correct.

Your Signature _____ Date _____
Spouse's Signature _____ Date _____

If any individual listed at the top of the IT-40 died *during* 2006, enter date of death below.
Taxpayer's date of death _____ 2006
Spouse's date of death _____ 2006

Paid Preparer's name
ADVANTAGE TAX PLUS
Address
2649 W. HORIZON RIDGE PKWY #120
City
HENDERSON
State NV   ZIP Code + 4 89052

☒ Federal ID Number   ☐ PTIN   **OR**   ☐ Social Security Number
30-0003336
Preparer's daytime telephone number
(702) 207-1040
Preparer's Signature   Date
Shin-Chi Chien, EA   08/07/2007

**Please mail to: Indiana Department of Revenue, P.O. Box 7231, Indianapolis, IN, 46207-7231**   Keep a copy for your records.

1030    IN|A0512 10/26/06

## Appendix B4-continued
# Schedule 1&2

---

| Schedules 1 & 2<br>Form IT-40, State Form 47908 R5 / 8-06 | Schedule 1: Indiana Deductions<br>(Schedule 2 begins after line 12 below) | Attachment<br>Sequence No. **01** |
|---|---|---|

Enter your first name, middle initial and last name and spouse's full name if filing a joint return

JEAN & BRAD SCOTT

Your Social Security Number   123-45-6789

### See Schedule 1 instructions

Please round all entries to nearest whole dollar (see instructions)

1  Renter's deduction: Address where rented if different from the one on page 1 of Form IT-40

_____

_____

Landlord's name and address _____

_____

_____ Amount of rent paid $_____

Number of months rented _____  Enter the lesser of $2,500 or amount of rent paid ......  | 1 | 0 0 |

2  Homeowner's residential property tax deduction: enter address where property tax was paid if different from page 1 of Form IT-40

_____

Enter the lesser of $2,500 or the actual amount of property tax paid for 2006 ........ Box A $  2,000.00

**Catch-Up Deduction**

Did you pay **2002** and/or **2003** property taxes in **2005**?

● Enter the amount of 2002 property taxes paid **during** 2005 (see instructions) ........................ Box B $  0 0

If yes, see instructions.

● Enter the amount of 2003 property taxes paid **during** 2005 (see instructions) ........................ Box C $  0 0

Add boxes A, B and C, enter the total here **(combined deduction cannot be more than $7,500)** ........ | 2 | 2,000.00 |

| 3 | State tax refund reported on federal return (see instructions) ............................. | 3 | 0 0 |
| 4 | Interest on U.S. government obligations (see instructions) ............................... | 4 | 0 0 |
| 5 | Taxable Social Security benefits (see instructions) ..................................... | 5 | 0 0 |
| 6 | Taxable railroad retirement benefits (see instructions) .................................. | 6 | 0 0 |
| 7 | Military service deduction: $2,000 maximum for qualifying person (see instructions) ........... | 7 | 0 0 |
| 8 | Non-Indiana locality earnings deduction: $2,000 maximum per qualifying person (see instructions) ...... | 8 | 0 0 |
| 9 | Insulation deduction: $1,000 maximum: attach verification (see instructions) ............... | 9 | 0 0 |
| 10 | Nontaxable portion of unemployment compensation (see instructions) .................... | 10 | 0 0 |

11  **Other Deductions:** See instructions (attach additional sheets if necessary)

| a | Enter deduction name _____ code no. ___ | 11a | 0 0 |
| b | Enter deduction name _____ code no. ___ | 11b | 0 0 |
| c | Enter deduction name _____ code no. ___ | 11c | 0 0 |
| d | Enter deduction name _____ code no. ___ | 11d | 0 0 |
| 12 | Add lines 1 through 11 and enter total on line 8 of Form IT-40 ............. **Total Deductions** ▶ | 12 | 2,000.00 |

---

### Schedule 2: Indiana Credits

| 1 | Credit for local taxes paid outside Indiana (see instructions) ............................. | 1 | 0 0 |
| 2 | County credit for the elderly: attach federal Schedule R (see instructions) .................. | 2 | 0 0 |

3  **Other Local Credits:** See instructions (attach additional sheets if necessary)

| a | Enter credit name _____ code no. ___ | 3a | 0 0 |
| b | Enter credit name _____ code no. ___ | b | 0 0 |

**Important:** Lines 1 through 3 cannot be greater than the county tax due on IT-40 line 17 (see instructions)

| 4 | College credit: attach Schedule CC-40 (see instructions) ................................ | 4 | 0 0 |
| 5 | Credit for taxes paid to other states: attach other state's return (see instructions) ........... | 5 | 0 0 |

6  **Other Credits:** See instructions (attach additional sheets if necessary)

| a | Enter credit name .... _____ code no. ___ | 6a | 0 0 |
| b | Enter credit name .... _____ code no. ___ | 6b | 0 0 |
| c | Enter credit name .... _____ code no. ___ | 6c | 0 0 |
| d | Enter credit name .... _____ code no. ___ | 6d | 0 0 |

**Important:** Lines 4 through 6 added together cannot be greater than the state adjusted gross income tax due on IT-40 line 16 (see instructions)

| 7 | Add lines 1 through 6 and enter total on line 29 of Form IT-40 ............. **Total Credits** ▶ | 7 | 0 0 |

1030                    INIA1401  10/24/06

## Appendix B4-continued
# Schedule IT-2210

| | | |
|---|---|---|
| **Schedule** **IT-2210** State Form 46002 R5 / 8-06 | **Indiana Department of Revenue** **2006 Underpayment of** **Estimated Tax by Individuals** Attach to Form IT-40, IT-40PNR or IT-40P | Attachment Sequence No. **06** |

Your first name and last name
JEAN                               SCOTT
Spouse's first name and last name (if filing a joint return)
BRAD                               SCOTT

Your Social Security Number 123-45-6789
Spouse's Social Security Number 234-56-7891

### Section A — Farmers and Fishermen Only — See Instructions

| | Annual Gross Income from All Sources | | Two-Thirds of Gross Income | Gross Income from Farming and Fishing |
|---|---|---|---|---|
| 2005 | 00 | x 66.7% = | 00 | 00 |
| 2006 | 00 | x 66.7% = | 00 | 00 |

**Section B:** **Early Filers** Check box if you filed your 2006 tax return and paid the total tax due by January 31, 2007. ☐

### Section C — Required Annual Payment

| | | | |
|---|---|---|---|
| 1 | 2006 tax | **1** | 2,448.00 |
| 2 | 2006 credits (not including withholding credits or estimated tax payments) | **2** | 00 |
| 3 | Subtract line 2 from line 1 | **3** | 2,448.00 |
| 4 | Multiply line 3 by 90% (.90) (farmers/fishermen multiply by .667, see instructions) ► | **4** | 2,203.00 |
| 5 | 2006 withholding tax credit | **5** | 00 |
| 6 | Subtract line 5 from line 3 — **If less than $400, STOP HERE! You do not owe a penalty** | **6** | 2,448.00 |
| 7 | Prior year's tax — **Read instructions** ► | **7** | 00 |
| 8 | Minimum required annual payment — Enter the lesser of line 4 or line 7 — **If less than or equal to the amount on line 5, STOP HERE! You do not owe a penalty** ► | **8** | 2,203.00 |

### Section D — Short Method — Read the instructions to determine if you can use the short method

| | | | |
|---|---|---|---|
| 9 | Enter the withholding tax credit amount from line 5 above | **9** | 00 |
| 10 | Enter the total amount, if any, of estimated tax payments you made for tax year 2006 | **10** | 00 |
| 11 | Add lines 9 and 10 | **11** | 00 |
| 12 | Total Underpayment. Subtract line 11 from line 8. If zero or less, **STOP HERE!** You do not owe a penalty. Attach this schedule to your tax return | **12** | 2,203.00 |
| 13 | Multiply line 12 by 10% (.10). Enter this amount on line 37 of Form IT-40 or line 33 of Form IT-40PNR | **13** | 220.00 |

### Section E — Regular Method

| | | | A 1st Installment April 17, 2006 | B 2nd Installment June 15, 2006 | C 3rd Installment September 15, 2006 | D 4th Installment January 16, 2007 |
|---|---|---|---|---|---|---|
| | | | **Installment Period Due Dates** | | | |
| 14 | Minimum required installment payment: divide amount on line 8 by 4 | **14** | 00 | 00 | 00 | 00 |
| 15 | 2006 withholding — Divide line 5 by 4 | **15** | 00 | 00 | 00 | 00 |
| **STOP!** | Complete lines 16 through 19 for each column before going to the next one. | | | | | |
| 16 | 2006 estimated taxes paid per period | **16** | 00 | 00 | 00 | 00 |
| 17 | Total installment payments (Add lines 15 and 16) | **17** | 00 | 00 | 00 | 00 |
| 18 | Installment period overpayment | **18** | 00 | 00 | 00 | 00 |
| 19 | Installment period underpayment | **19** | 00 | 00 | 00 | 00 |
| 20 | Total underpayment — Add line 19, Columns A + B + C + D and enter total here | **20** | | | | 00 |
| 21 | Underpayment penalty — Multiply line 20 by 10% (.10). Enter this amount on line 37 of Form IT-40 or line 33 of Form IT-40PNR ► | **21** | | | | 00 |

1030                                         INAC0201   09/21/06

# Appendix C
# Basic IRS Information for Gamblers
# Revenue Procedure 77-29

## SECTION 1—PURPOSE

The purpose of this revenue procedure is to provide guidelines to taxpayers concerning the treatment of wagering gains and losses for Federal income tax purposes and the related responsibility for maintaining adequate records in support of winnings and losses.

## SECTION 2—BACKGROUND

Income derived from wagering transactions is includible in gross income under the provisions of section 61 of the Internal Revenue Code of 1954. Losses from wagering transactions are allowable only to the extent of gains from such transactions, under section 165(d) of the Code, and may be claimed only as an itemized deduction.

Temporary regulations section 7.6041-1 (T.D. 7492, 1977-2 C.B. 463), effective May 1, 1977, require all persons in a trade or business who, in the course of that trade or business, make any payment of

$1,200 or more in winnings from a bingo game or slot machine play, or $1,500 or more in winnings from a keno game, to prepare Form W-2G, Statement for Certain Gambling Winnings, for each person to whom the winnings are paid.

In determining whether such winnings equal or exceed the $1,500 reporting floor and in determining the amount to be reported on Form W-2G in the case of a keno game, the amount of winnings from any one game shall be reduced by the amount wagered for that one game. In the case of bingo or slot machines, the total winnings will not be reduced by the amount wagered. Forms W-2G reporting such payments must be filed with the Internal Revenue Service on or before February 28 following the year of payment.

Winnings of $600 or more, unreduced by the amount of the wagers, must also be reported for every person paid gambling winnings from horse racing, dog racing, or jai alai, if such winnings are at least 300 times the amount wagered.

Winnings of $600 or more, unreduced by the amount of the wagers, must also be reported for every person paid gambling winnings from state conducted lotteries.

Under Section 6001 of the Code, taxpayers must keep records necessary to verify items reported on their income tax returns. Records supporting items on a tax return should be retained until the statute of limitations on that return expires.

## SECTION 3—PROCEDURES

An accurate diary or similar record regularly maintained by the taxpayer, supplemented by verifiable documentation will usually be acceptable evidence for substantiation of wagering winnings and losses. In general, the diary should contain at least the following information:

1) Date and type of specific wager or wagering activity;
2) Name of gambling establishment;

3) Address or location of gambling establishment;

4) Name(s) of other person(s) (if any) present with taxpayer at gambling establishment; and

5) Amount(s) won or lost.

Verifiable documentation for gambling transactions includes but is not limited to Forms W-2G; Forms 5754, Statement by Person Receiving Gambling Winnings; wagering tickets, canceled checks, credit records, bank withdrawals, and statements of actual winnings or payment slips provided to the taxpayer by the gambling establishment.

Where possible, the diary and available documentation generated with the placement and settlement of a wager should be further supported by other documentation of the taxpayer's wagering activity or visit to a gambling establishment. Such documentation includes, but is not limited to, hotel bills, airline tickets, gasoline credit cards, canceled checks, credit records, bank deposits, and bank withdrawals.

Additional supporting evidence could also include affidavits or testimony from responsible gambling officials regarding wagering activity.

The Service is required to report to the Congress by 1979 on the issue of whether casino winnings should be subject to withholding. In the absence of legislation requiring withholding on casino winnings, the instructions for preparing Form 5754 will not be applicable to winnings from keno, bingo, or slot machines. However, all other items of documentation to verify gambling losses from casino winnings are applicable.

With regard to specific wagering transactions, winnings and losses may be further supported by the following items:

**.01 Keno**—Copies of keno tickets purchased by the taxpayer and validated by the gambling establishment, copies of the taxpayer's casino credit records, and copies of the taxpayer's casino check cashing records.

**.02 Slot Machines**—A record of all winnings by date and time that the machine was played. (In Nevada, the machine number is the number required by the State Gaming Commission and may or may not be displayed in a prominent place on the machine. If not displayed on the machine, the number may be requested from the casino operator.)

**.03 Table Games**—Twenty One (Blackjack), Craps, Poker, Baccarat, Roulette, Wheel of Fortune, Etc.—The number of the table at which the taxpayer was playing. Casino credit card data indicating whether the credit was issued in the pit or at the cashier's cage.

**.04 Bingo**—A record of the number of games played, cost of tickets purchased and amounts collected on winning tickets. Supplemental records include any receipts from the casino, parlor, etc.

**.05 Racing**—Horse, Harness, Dog, Etc.—A record of the races, entries amounts of wagers, and amounts collected on winning tickets and amounts lost on losing tickets. Supplemental records include unredeemed tickets and payment records from the racetrack.

**.06 Lotteries**—A record of ticket purchases, dates, winnings and losses. Supplemental records include unredeemed tickets, payment slips and winnings statement.

# SECTION 4—LIMITATIONS

The record-keeping suggestions set forth above are intended as general guidelines to assist taxpayers in establishing their reportable gambling gains and deductible gambling losses. While following these will enable most taxpayers to meet their obligations under the Internal Revenue Code these guidelines cannot be all inclusive and the tax liability of each depends on the facts and circumstances of particular situations.

*This is the landmark Supreme Court case (1987) that
allowed gamblers to file as professionals. What's interesting about this case is that the tax deficiency was a
puny $2,522 and Robert Groetzinger acted as his own
lawyer. Now there's one persistent man!*

# Appendix D

## THE GROETZINGER CASE
## GAMBLING AS A BUSINESS

Commissioner v. Groetzinger, KTC 1987-123 (S.Ct. 1987)
SUPREME COURT OF THE UNITED STATES
COMMISSIONER OF INTERNAL REVENUE,
Petitioner v. ROBERT P. GROETZINGER,
Respondent. Docket: 85-1226 Filed February 24, 1987

## SYLLABUS

Certiorari To The United States Court Of Appeals For The Seventh Circuit

For most of 1978, respondent devoted 60 to 80 hours per week
to pari-mutuel wagering on dog races with a view to earning a living from such activity, had no other employment, and gambled solely

for his own account. His efforts generated gross winnings of $70,000 on bets of $72,032, for a net gambling loss for the year of $2,032. Although he reported this loss on his 1978 tax return, he did not utilize it in computing his adjusted gross income or claim it as a deduction. Upon audit, the Commissioner of Internal Revenue determined that, under the Internal Revenue Code of 1954 (Code) as it existed in 1978, respondent was subject to a minimum tax because part of the gambling loss deduction to which he was entitled was an "item of tax preference." Under the Code, such items could be lessened by certain deductions that were "attributable to a trade or business carried on by the taxpayer." In redetermining respondent's tax deficiency, the Tax Court held that he was in the "trade or business" of gambling, so that no part of his gambling losses were an item of tax preference subjecting him to a minimum tax for 1978. The Court of Appeals affirmed.

Held: A full-time gambler who makes wagers solely for his own account is engaged in a "trade or business" within the meaning of Code sections 162(a) and 62(1). 771 F.2d 269, affirmed. OPINION

BLACKMUN, J., delivered the opinion of the Court, in which BRENNAN, MARSHALL, POWELL, STEVENS, and O'CONNOR, JJ., joined. WHITE, J., filed a dissenting opinion, in which REHNQUIST, C.J., and SCALIA, J., joined.

The issue in this case is whether a full-time gambler who makes wagers solely for his own account is engaged in a "trade or business," within the meaning of section 162(a) and 62(1) of the Internal Revenue Code of 1954, as amended, 26 U.S.C. sections 162(a) and 62(1).

The tax year with which we here are concerned is the calendar year 1978; technically, then, we look to the Code as it read at that time.

I. There is no dispute as to the facts. The critical ones are stipulated. See App. 9. Respondent Robert P. Groetzinger had worked for 20 years in sales and market research for an Illinois manufacturer when his position was terminated in February 1978. During the remainder of that year, respondent busied himself with pari-mutuel wagering, primarily on greyhound races. He gambled at tracks in Florida and Colorado. He went to the track 6 days a week for 48 weeks in

1978. He spent a substantial amount of time studying racing forms, programs, and other materials. He devoted from 60 to 80 hours each week to these gambling-related endeavors. He never placed bets on behalf of any other person, or sold tips, or collected commissions for placing bets, or functioned as a bookmaker. He gambled solely for his own account. He had no other profession or type of employment.

Respondent kept a detailed accounting of his wagers and every day noted his winnings and losses in a record book. In 1978, he had gross winnings of $70,000, but he bet $72,032; he thus realized a net gambling loss for the year of $2,032.

Respondent received $6,498 in income from other sources in 1978. This came from interest, dividends, capital gains, and salary earned before his job was terminated.

On the federal income tax return he filed for the calendar year 1978 respondent reported as income only the $6,498 realized from non-gambling sources. He did not report any gambling winnings or deduct any gambling losses.

He did not itemize deductions. Instead, he computed his tax liability from the tax tables.

Upon audit, the Commissioner of Internal Revenue determined that respondent's $70,000 in gambling winnings were to be included in his gross income and that, pursuant to section 165(d) of the Code, 26 U.S.C. section 165(d), a deduction was to be allowed for his gambling losses to the extent of these gambling gains. But the Commissioner further determined that, under the law as it was in 1978, a portion of respondent's $70,000 gambling-loss deduction was an item of tax preference and operated to subject him to the minimum tax under section 56(a) of the Code, 26 U.S.C. section 56(a) (1976 ed.). At that time, under statutory provisions in effect from 1976 until 1982, "items of tax preference" were lessened by certain deductions, but not by deductions not "attributable to a trade or business carried on by the taxpayer." sections 57(a)(1) and (b)(1)(A), and section 62(1), 26 U.S.C. sections 57(a)(1) and (b)(1)(A), and section 62(1) (1976 ed. and Supp. I).

These determinations by the Commissioner produced a section

56(a) minimum tax of $2,142 and, with certain other adjustments not now in dispute, resulted in a total asserted tax deficiency of $2,522 for respondent for 1978.

Respondent sought redetermination of the deficiency in the United States Tax Court. That court, in a reviewed decision, with only two judges dissenting, held that respondent was in the trade or business of gambling, and that, as a consequence, no part of his gambling losses constituted an item of tax preference in determining any minimum tax for 1978. 82 T.C. 793 (1984). In so ruling, the court adhered to its earlier court-reviewed decision in Ditunno v. Commissioner, 80 T.C. 362 (1983). The court in Ditunno, id., at 371, had overruled Gentile v. Commissioner, 65 T.C. 1 (1975), a case where it had rejected the Commissioner's contention (contrary to his position here) that a full-time gambler was in a trade or business and therefore was subject to self-employment tax.

The United States Court of Appeals for the Seventh Circuit affirmed. 771 F.2d 269 (1985). Because of a conflict on the issue among the Courts of Appeals, we granted certiorari. ____ U.S. ____ (1986).


II. The phrase "trade or business" has been in section 162(a) and in that section's predecessors for many years. Indeed, the phrase is common in the Code, for it appears in over 50 sections and 800 subsections and in hundreds of places in proposed and final income tax regulations. The slightly longer phrases, "carrying on a trade or business" and "engaging in a trade or business," themselves are used no less than 60 times in the Code. The concept thus has a well-known and almost constant presence on our tax-law terrain. Despite this, the Code has never contained a definition of the words "trade or business" for general application, and no regulation has been issued expounding its meaning for all purposes.

Neither has a broadly applicable authoritative judicial definition emerged.

Our task in this case is to ascertain the meaning of the phrase as it appears in the sections of the Code with which we are here concerned.

In one of its early tax cases, Flint v. Stone Tracy Co., 220 U.S. 107-1 (1911), the Court was concerned with the Corporation Tax imposed by the Tariff Act of 1909, 36 Stat., ch. 6, 11, 112-117, and the status of being engaged in business. It said: "'Business' is a very comprehensive term and embraces everything about which a person can be employed." 220 U.S., at 171. It embraced the Bouvier Dictionary definition: "That which occupies the time, attention and labor of men for the purpose of a livelihood or profit." Ibid. See also Helvering v. Horst, 311 U.S. 112, 1181 (1940). And Justice Frankfurter has observed that "we assume that Congress uses common words in their popular meaning, as used in the common speech of men." Frankfurter, Some Reflections on the Reading of Statutes, 47 Colum. L. Rev. 527, 536 (1947).

With these general comments as significant background, we turn to pertinent cases decided here. Snyder v. Commissioner, 295 U.S. 134 (1935), had to do with margin trading and capital gains, and held, in that context, that an investor, seeking merely to increase his holdings, was not engaged in a trade or business. Justice Brandeis, in his opinion for the Court, noted that the Board of Tax Appeals theretofore had ruled that a taxpayer who devoted the major portion of his time to transactions on the stock exchange for the purpose of making a livelihood could treat losses incurred as having been sustained in the course of a trade or business. He went on to observe that no facts were adduced in Snyder to show that the taxpayer "might properly be characterized as a 'trader on an exchange who makes a living in buying and selling securities.'" Id., at 139. These observations, thus, are dicta, but, by their use, the Court appears to have drawn a distinction between an active trader and an investor.

In Deputy v. duPont, 308 U.S. 488 (1940), the Court was concerned with what were "ordinary and necessary" expenses of a taxpayer's trade or business, within the meaning of section 23(a) of the Revenue Act of 1928, 45 Stat. 799. In ascertaining whether carrying charges on short sales of stock were deductible as ordinary and necessary expenses of the taxpayer's business, the Court assumed that the activities of the taxpayer in conserving and enhancing his estate constituted a trade or business, but nevertheless disallowed the claimed deductions because they were not "ordinary" or "necessary." 308 U.S., at 493-497. Justice Frankfurter, in a concurring opinion joined by Justice Reed, did not join the majority. He took the position that whether the taxpayer's activities constituted a trade or business was "open for determination," id., at 499, and observed:

"'... carrying on any trade or business,' within the contemplation of section 23(a), involves holding one's self out to others as engaged in the selling of goods or services. This the taxpayer did not do. ... Without elaborating the reasons for this construction and not unmindful of opposing considerations, including appropriate regard for administrative practice, I prefer to make the conclusion explicit instead of making the hypothetical litigation-breeding assumption that this taxpayer's activities, for which expenses were sought to be deducted, did constitute a 'trade or business.'" Ibid.

Next came Higgins v. Commissioner, 312 U.S. 212 (1941). There the Court, in a bare and brief unanimous opinion, ruled that salaries and other-expenses incident to looking after one's own investments in bonds and stocks were not deductible under section 23(a) of the Revenue Act of 1932, 47 Stat. 179, as expenses paid or incurred in carrying on a trade or business. While surely cutting back on Flint's broad approach, the Court seemed to do little more than announce that since 1918 "the present form [of the statute] was fixed and has so continued"; that "no regulation has ever been promulgated which interprets the meaning of 'carrying on a business'"; that the comprehensive definition of "business" in Flint was "not controlling in this dissimilar inquiry"; that the facts in each case must be examined; that not all expenses of every business transaction are deductible; and that "[n]o matter how large the estate or how continuous or extended the work required may be, such facts are not sufficient as a matter of law to permit the courts to reverse the decision of the Board." 312 U.S., at 215-218. The opinion, therefore,—although devoid of analysis and not setting forth what elements, if any, in addition to profit motive and regularity, were required to render an activity a trade or business—must stand for the propositions that full-time market activity in managing and preserving one's own estate is not embraced within the phrase "carrying on a business," and that salaries and other expenses incident to the operation are not deductible as having been paid or incurred in a trade or business.

See also United States v. Gilmore, 372 U.S. 39, 44-45 (1963); Whipple v. Commissioner, 373 U.S. 193 (1963). It is of interest to note that, although Justice Frankfurter was on the Higgins Court and this time did not write separately, and although Justice Reed, who had joined the concurring opinion in duPont, was the author of the Higgins opinion, the Court in that case did not even cite duPont and thus paid no heed whatsoever to the content of Justice Frankfurter's pronouncement in his concurring opinion.

Adoption of the Frankfurter gloss obviously would have disposed of the case in the Commissioner's favor handily and automatically, but that easy route was not followed.

Less than three months later, the Court considered the issue of the deductibility, as business expenses, of estate and trust fees. In unanimous opinions issued the same day and written by Justice Black, the Court ruled that the efforts of an estate or trust in asset conservation and maintenance did not constitute a trade or business. City Bank Farmers Trust Co. v. Helvering, 313 U.S. 121 (1941); United States v. Pyne, 313 U.S. 127 (1941). The Higgins case was deemed to be relevant and controlling. Again, no mention was made of the Frankfurter concurrence in duPont. Yet Justices Reed and Frankfurter were on the Court.

Snow v. Commissioner, 416 U.S. 500 (1974), concerned a taxpayer who had advanced capital to a partnership formed to develop an invention. On audit of his 1966 return, a claimed deduction under section 174(a)(1) of the 1954 Code for his pro rata share of the partnership's operating loss was disallowed. The Tax Court and the Sixth Circuit upheld that disallowance. This Court reversed. Justice Douglas, writing for the eight Justices who participated, observed: "Section 174 was enacted in 1954 to dilute some of the conception of 'ordinary and necessary' business expenses under section 162(a) (then section 23(a)(1) of the Internal Revenue Code of 1939) adumbrated by Mr. Justice Frankfurter in a concurring opinion in Deputy v. duPont ... where he said that the section in question ... "involves holding one's self out to others as engaged in the selling of goods or services." 416 U.S., at 502-503. He went on to state, id., at 503, that section 162(a) "is more narrowly written than is section 174."

From these observations and decisions, we conclude (1) that, to be sure, the statutory words are broad and comprehensive (Flint); (2) that, however, expenses incident to caring for one's own investments, even though that endeavor is full-time, are not deductible as paid or incurred in carrying on a trade or business (Higgins; City Bank; Pyne); (3) that the opposite conclusion may follow for an active trader (Snyder); (4) that Justice Frankfurter's attempted gloss upon the decision in duPont was not adopted by the Court in that case; (5) that the Court, indeed, later characterized it as an "adumbration" (Snow); and (6) that the Frankfurter observation, specifically or by implication, never has been accepted as law by a majority opinion of the Court, and more than once has been totally ignored. We must regard the Frankfurter gloss merely as a two-Justice pronouncement in a passing moment, and, while entitled to respect, as never having achieved the status of a Court ruling. One also must acknowledge that Higgins, with its stress on examining the facts in each case, affords no readily helpful standard, in the usual sense, with which to decide the present case and others similar to it. The Court's cases, thus, give us results, but little general guidance.

III. Federal and state legislation and court decisions, perhaps understandably, until recently have not been noticeably favorable to gambling endeavors and even have been reluctant to treat gambling on a parity with more "legitimate" means of making a living. See, e.g., sections 4401 et seq. of the Code; Marchetti v. United States, 390 U.S. 39, 44-46, and nn. 5 and 6 (1968).

And the confinement of gambling-loss deductions to the amount of gambling gains, a provision brought into the income tax law as section 23(g) of the Revenue Act of 1934, 48 Stat. 689, and carried forward into section 165(d) of the 1954 Code, closed the door on suspected abuses, see H.R. Rep. No. 704, 73d Cong., 2d Sess., 22 (1934);

S. Rep. No. 558, 73d Cong., 2 Sess., 25 (1934), but served partially to differentiate genuine gambling losses from many other types of adverse financial consequences sustained during the tax year. Gambling winnings, however, have not been isolated from gambling losses. The Congress has been realistic enough to recognize that such losses do exist and do have some effect on income, which is the primary focus of the federal income tax.

The issue this case presents has "been around" for a long time and, as indicated above, has not met with consistent treatment in the Tax Court itself or in the Federal Courts of Appeals. The Seventh Circuit, in the present case, said the issue "has proven to be most difficult and troublesome over the years." 771 F.2d, at 271. The difficulty has not been ameliorated by the persistent absence of an all-purpose definition, by statute or regulation, of the phrase "trade or business" which so frequently appears in the Code. Of course, this very frequency well may be the explanation for legislative and administrative reluctance to take a position as to one use that might affect, with confusion, so many others.

Be that as it may, this taxpayer's case must be decided and, from what we have outlined above, must be decided in the face of a decisional history that is not positive or even fairly indicative, as we read the cases, of what the result should be. There are, however, some helpful indicators.

If a taxpayer, as Groetzinger is stipulated to have done in 1978, devotes his full-time activity to gambling, and it is his intended livelihood source, it would seem that basic concepts of fairness (if there be much of that in the income tax law) demand that his activity be regarded as a trade or business just as any other readily accepted activity, such as being a retail store proprietor or, to come closer categorically, as being a casino operator or as being an active trader on the exchanges.

It is argued, however, that a full-time gambler is not offering goods or his services, within the line of demarcation that Justice Frankfurter would have drawn in duPont. Respondent replies that he indeed is supplying goods and services, not only to himself but, as well, to the gambling market; thus, he says, he comes within the Frankfurter test even if that were to be imposed as the proper measure. "It takes two to gamble." Brief for Respondent 3. Surely, one who clearly satisfies the Frankfurter adumbration usually is in a trade or business. But does it necessarily follow that one who does not satisfy the Frankfurter adumbration is not in a trade or business? One might well feel that a full-time gambler ought to qualify as much as a full-time trader, as Justice Brandeis in Snyder implied and as courts have held.

The Commissioner, indeed, accepts the trader result. Tr. of Oral Arg. 17. In any event, while the offering of goods and services usually would qualify the activity as a trade or business, this factor, it seems to us, is not an absolute prerequisite.

We are not satisfied that the Frankfurter gloss would add any helpful dimension to the resolution of cases such as this one, or that it provides a "sensible test," as the Commissioner urges. See Brief for Petitioner 36. It might assist now and then, when the answer is obvious and positive, but it surely is capable of breeding litigation over the meaning of "goods," the meaning of "services," or the meaning of "holding one's self out." And we suspect that—apart from gambling—almost every activity would satisfy the gloss.

A test that everyone passes is not a test at all. We therefore now formally reject the Frankfurter gloss which the Court has never adopted anyway.

Of course, not every income-producing and profit-making endeavor constitutes a trade or business. The income tax law, almost from the beginning, has distinguished between a business or trade, on the one hand, and "transactions entered into for profit but not connected with ... business or trade," on the other. See Revenue Act of 1916, section 5(a) Fifth, 39 Stat. 759. Congress "distinguished the broad range of income or profit producing activities from those satisfying the narrow category of trade or business." Whipple v. Commissioner, 373 U.S. 193, 197 (1963). We accept the fact that to be engaged in a trade or business, the taxpayer must be involved in the activity with continuity and regularity and that the taxpayer's primary purpose for engaging in the activity must be for income or profit. A sporadic activity, a hobby, or an amusement diversion does not qualify.

It is suggested that we should defer to the position taken by the Commissioner and by the Solicitor General, but, in the absence of guidance, for over several decades now, through the medium of definitive statutes or regulations, we see little reason to do so. We would defer, instead, to the Code's normal focus on what we regard as a common-sense concept of what is a trade or business. Otherwise, as here, in the context of a minimum tax, it is not too extreme to say that the taxpayer is being taxed on his gambling losses, a result distinctly out of line with the Code's focus on income.

We do not overrule or cut back on the Court's holding in Higgins when we conclude that if one's gambling activity is pursued full time, in good faith, and with regularity, to the production of income for a livelihood, and is not a mere hobby, it is a trade or business within the meaning of the statutes with which we are here concerned. Respondent Groetzinger satisfied that test in 1978. Constant and large-scale effort on his part was made. Skill was required and was applied. He did what he did for a livelihood, though with a less than successful result. This was not a hobby or a passing fancy or an occasional bet for amusement.

We therefore adhere to the general position of the Higgins Court, taken 45 years ago, that resolution of this issue "requires an examination of the facts in each case." 312 U.S., at 217. This may be thought by some to be a less-than-satisfactory solution, for facts vary. See Boyle, What is a Trade or Business?, 39 Tax Lawyer 737, 767 (1986); Note, The Business of Betting: Proposals for Reforming the Taxation of Business Gamblers, 38 Tax Lawyer 759 (1985); Lopez, Defining "Trade of Business" under the Internal Revenue Code: A Survey of Relevant Cases, 11 Fla. St. L. Rev. 949 (1984). Cf. Comment, Continuing Vitality of the "Goods or Services" Test, 15 U. Balt. L. Rev. 108 (1985). But the difficulty rests in the Code's wide utilization in various contexts of the term "trade or business," in the absence of an all-purpose definition by statute or regulation, and in our concern that an attempt judicially to formulate and impose a test for all situations would be counterproductive, unhelpful, and even somewhat precarious for the overall integrity of the Code. We leave repair or revision, if any be needed, which we doubt, to the Congress where we feel, at this late date, the ultimate responsibility rests. Cf. Flood v. Kuhn, 407 U.S. 258, 269-285 (1972).

The judgment of the Court of Appeals is affirmed.

It is so ordered.

Justice WHITE, with whom The Chief Justice and Justice SCA-LIA join, dissenting.

The 1982 amendments to the Tax Code made clear that gambling is not a trade or business. Under those amendments, the alternative minimum tax base equals adjusted gross income reduced by specified amounts, including gambling losses, and increased by items not relevant here. See 26 U.S.C. sections 55(b), 55(e)(1)(A), 165(d) (1982 ed. and Supp. III).

If full-time gambling were a trade or business, a full-time gambler's gambling losses would be "deductions ... attributable to a trade or business carried on by the taxpayer," and hence deductible from gross income in computing adjusted gross income, 26 U.S.C. section 62((1), though only to the extent of gambling winnings, 26 U.S.C. section 165(d). To again subtract gambling losses (to the extent of gambling winnings) from adjusted gross income when computing the alternative minimum tax base would be to give the full-time gambler a double deduction for alternative minimum tax purposes, which was certainly not Congress' intent.

Thus, when Congress amended the alternative minimum tax provisions in 1982, it implicitly accepted the teaching of Gentile v. Commissioner, 65 T.C. 1 (1975), that gambling is not a trade or business.

Groetzinger would have had no problem under the 1982 amendments.

One could argue, I suppose, that although gambling is not a trade or business under the 1982 amendments, it was in 1978, the tax year at issue here. But there is certainly no indication that Congress intended in 1982 to alter the status of gambling as a trade or business. Rather, Congress was correcting an inequity that had arisen because gambling is not a trade or business, just as 40 years earlier Congress had, by enacting the predecessor to 26 U.S.C. section 212, corrected an inequity that became apparent when this Court held that a full-time investor is not engaged in a trade or business. See Higgins v. Commissioner, 312 U.S. 212 (1941). In neither case did Congress attempt to alter the then-prevailing definition of trade or business, nor do I think this Court should do so now to avoid a harsh result in this case.

In any event the Court should recognize that its holding is a sport that applies only to a superseded statute and not to the tax years governed by the 1982 amendments. Accordingly, I dissent.

## MAJORITY OPINION

1. All references herein to the Internal Revenue Code are, unless otherwise described, to the 1954 Code, not to the Internal Revenue Code of 1986, as it has been designated by section 2(a) of the Tax Reform Act of 1986, _____ Stat. _____.

2. The Tax Court put it this way: "It is not disputed that petitioner during 1978 was engaged full-time in parimutuel wagering on dog races, had no other employment during that period, gambled solely for his own account, and devoted an extraordinary amount of time and effort to his gambling with a view to earning a living from such activity." 82 T.C. 793, 796 (1984).

3. Respondent, however, did report his net gambling loss of $2,032 in Schedule E (Supplemental Income Schedule) of his return, but he did not utilize that amount in computing his adjusted gross income or claim it as an itemized deduction.

4. This statutory scheme was amended by the Tax Equity and Fiscal Responsibility Act of 1982, section 201(a), 96 Stat. 411. For tax years after 1982, gambling-loss deductions explicitly are excluded from the minimum tax base. The Commissioner acknowledges that a taxpayer like respondent for a year after 1982 would not be subject to minimum tax liability because of his gambling-loss deduction. Brief for Petitioner 4, n. 4.

5. Compare Nipper v. Commissioner, 746 F.2d 813 (CA11 1984), affg, without opinion, 47 TCM 136, paragraph 83.644 P-H Memo TC (1983), and the Seventh Circuit's decision in the present case, with Gajewski v. Commissioner, 723 F.2d 1062 (CA2 1983), cert. denied, 469 U.S. 818 (1984); Estate of Cull v. Commissioner, 746 F.2d 1148 (CA6 1984), cert. denied, 472 U.S. 1007 (1985), and Noto v. United States, 770 F.2d 1073 (CA3 1985), affg, without opinion, 598 F. Supp. 4404 (NJ 1984).

Despite the interim reversals by the Second and Sixth Circuits in Gajewski and Cull, supra, the Tax Court has adhered to its position that a full-time gambler is engaged in a trade or business. See, e.g., Meredith v. Commissioner, 49 TCM 318, paragraph 84,651 P-H Memo TC (1984); Barrish v. Commissioner, 49 TCM 115, paragraph 84,602 P-H Memo TC (1984). It has drawn no distinction between the gambler and the active market trader. See also Baxter v. United States, 688 F. Supp. 912 (Nev. 1986).

6. Some sections of the Code, however, do define the term for limited purposes. See section 355(b)(2), 26 U.S.C. section 355(b)(2) (distribution of stock of controlled corporation); sections 502(b) and 513(b), 26 U.S.C. sections 502(b) and 513(b) (exempt organizations), and section 7701(a)(26), 26 U.S.C. section 7701(a)(26) (defining the term to include "the performance of the functions of a public office").

7. Judge Friendly some time ago observed that "the courts have properly assumed that the term includes all means of gaining a livelihood by work, even those which would scarcely be so characterized in common speech." Trent v. Commissioner, 291 F.2d 669, 671 (CA2 1961).

8. We caution that in this opinion our interpretation of the phrase "trade or business" is confined to the specific sections of the Code at issue here. We do not purport to construe the phrase where it appears in other places.

9. See, however, section 212 of the 1954 Code, 26 U.S.C. section 212. This section has its roots in section 23(a)(2) of the 1939 Code, as added by section 121 of the Revenue Act of 1942, 56 Stat. 819. It allows as a deduction all the ordinary and necessary expenses paid or

incurred "for the management, conservation, or maintenance of property held for the production of income," and thus overcame the specific ruling in Higgins that expenses of that kind were not deductible. The statutory change, of course, does not read directly on the term "trade or business." Obviously, though, Congress sought to overcome Higgins and achieved that end.

10. Deputy v. duPont, 308 U.S. 488 (1940), however, was cited by the parties in their Higgins briefs submitted to this Court. See Brief for Petitioner 28, 29, 40 and 61, and Brief for Respondent 17 and 18, in Higgins v. Commissioner, O.T. 1940, No. 253.

11. Today, however, the vast majority of States permit some form of public gambling. The lottery, bingo, parimutuel betting, jai alai, casinos, and slot machines easily come to mind.

12. "It takes a buyer to make a seller and it takes an opposing gambler to make a bet." Boyle, What is a Trade or Business?, 39 Tax Lawyer 737, 763 (1986).

13. Levin v. United States, 597 F.2d 760, 765 (Ct. Cl. 1979); Commissioner v. Nubar, 185 F.2d 584, 588 (CA4 1950), cert. denied, 341 U.S. 925 (1961); Fuld v. Commissioner, 189 F.2d 465, 468-469 (CA2 1943). See also Moller v. United States, 721 F.2d 810 (CA Fed. 1983), cert. denied, 467 U.S. 1251 (1984); Purvis v. Commissioner, 580 F.2d 1882, 1884 (CA9 1976).

14. Each of the three cases in conflict with the Seventh Circuit's decision in the present case, see n. 5, supra, was a gambler's case and adopted the Frankfurter gloss. Because the same courts, in cases not involving gamblers, have not referred to the Frankfurter gloss, see Bessenyey v. Commissioner, 379 F.2d 252 (CA2), cert. denied, 389 U.S. 981 (1967); Gestrich v. Commissioner, 681 F.2d 805 (CA3 1982), aff'g, without opinion, 74 T.C. 525 (1980), Main Line Distributors, Inc. v. Commissioner, 321 F.2d 562 (CA6 1963), it would appear that these courts in effect were creating a special class of, and with special rules for, the full-time gambler. We find no warrant for this in the Code.

15. "The more he lost, the more minimum tax he has to pay." Boyle, 39 Tax Lawyer, at 754. The Commissioner concedes that ap-

plication of the goods-or-services-test here "visits somewhat harsh consequences" on taxpayer Groetzinger, Brief for Petitioner 36, and "points to ... perhaps unfortunate draftsmanship." Ibid. See also Reply Brief for Petitioner 11.

16. It is possible, of course, that our conclusion here may subject the gambler to self-employment tax, see sections 1401-1403 of the Code, and therefore may not be an unmixed blessing for him. Federal taxes, however, rest where Congress has placed them.

## JUDGE WHITE'S DISSENTING OPINION

1. All references are to the Code as it stood prior to the 1986 amendments.

2. Consider two single individuals filing for the tax year ending December 31, 1986: A has $75,000 in nongambling income, and $75,000 in itemized nongambling deductions; B, a full-time gambler, has $75,000 in gambling winnings, $75,000 in gambling losses, $75,000 in nongambling income, and $75,000 in itemized nongambling deductions. A's gross income and adjusted gross income are both $75,000, and so is his alternative minimum tax base. The alternative minimum tax assessed on A is 20% of the excess of $75,000 over $30,000, see 26 U.S.C. sections 55(a), 55(f)(1)(B), or $9,000.00. Assuming that full-time gambling is a trade or business, B has gross income of $150,000, adjusted gross income of $75,000 (because his gambling losses are attributable to a trade or business), and an alternative minimum tax base of zero (because gambling losses are deducted from adjusted gross income in computing the alternative minimum tax base). Thus, if full-time gambling were treated as a trade or business, B's gambling losses would shield him against the $9,000 minimum tax that Congress clearly intended him to pay. "The Code should not be interpreted to allow [a taxpayer] 'the practical equivalent of a double deduction.' Charles Ilfeld Co. v. Hernandez, 292 U.S. 62, 68 (1934), absent a clear declaration of intent by Congress." United

States v. Skelly Oil Co., 394 U.S. 678, 684 (1969). There is no such clear declaration of intent accompanying the 1982 amendments.

3. The Commissioner had acquiesced in Gentile. See 1980-2 Cum. Bull. 1, 4, n. 39.

4. While the consequences of accepting the Commissioner's position in this case may be harsh to the respondent—which is no doubt why Congress amended the relevant Code provisions in 1982—I find the Court's characterization of the result as a tax on gambling losses, ante, at ____, somewhat misleading. If gambling is not a trade or business, the practical effect of the minimum tax on tax preference items is to reduce the deduction allowed for gambling losses from an amount equal to 100% of gambling winnings to some lesser percentage of gambling winnings.

# About the Authors

## JEAN SCOTT

Jean Scott is the author of three books in the Frugal Gambler series. She's a writer, speaker, and television personality, a veritable spokesperson for low-rolling gamblers nationwide. She lives in Las Vegas with her husband Brad. Her website is www.queenofcomps. com.

## MARISSA CHIEN

Marissa Chien is an Enrolled Agent and the president of her own firm, Advantage Tax Plus, Inc, where she provides tax accounting, financial planning, and wealth management services to her clients. She is a graduate of the University of Michigan and has approximately 300 individual and corporate clients, including Jean Scott and Phil Gordon as well as other poker champions and professional gamblers. She has limited availability for private consultations and can be reached at 702/207-1040 or advantagetaxplus@aol.com.

# ABOUT HUNTINGTON PRESS

Huntington Press is a specialty publisher of Las
Vegas- and gambling-related books and periodicals,
including the award-winning consumer newsletter,
*Anthony Curtis' Las Vegas Advisor.*

Huntington Press
3665 South Procyon Avenue
Las Vegas, Nevada 89103